Cyril Passfield

Out West

a novel
by
John Passfield

Rock's Mills Press
Oakville, Ontario
2019

Published by
Rock's Mills Press
www.rocksmillspress.com

Copyright © 2019 John Passfield.
All rights reserved. Published by arrangement with the author.

No part of this book may be reproduced, stored in a retrieval system, or transmitted by any means without the written permission of the author.

ISBN-13: 978-1-77244-168-0

Cover Design: Craig Passfield.

Cover Illustration: A photo of Charlie Thompson (left) and Cyril Passfield (right) lighting a fire while 'on the hobo' in Western Canada in the summer of 1932.

Author's Website: www.johnpassfield.ca

Chapter 1

Swimming with Charlie at Pinafore Park. Shaking the water off as we stand beside the dock. Lying on the grass across the pond from the ice cream pavilion and talking. How neither one of us is getting much time on the railroad. Even if somebody's sick, there's a whole whack of guys they call in first before they call us. It's seniority, and with the way things are going with this economy there's going to be a lot less work if they have another round of lay-offs again. Talking about the old ice-house. Used to be lots of work over there when we were kids. So what do you think we oughta do to get some work?

Slept in boxcar.

Two boys towelling off after a swim.
A dying man with a gargle in his throat.
A young boy jouncing along on his father's shoulders.

Had hazardous time.

A bread line stretching the length of a block.
Hail bouncing on a cedar-shingle roof.
A dust cloud blotting out a prairie sky.

Jumped an empty.

Where are you going?
Where have you been?
Where are you now?

12:00 - 12:01 - 12:02 - 12:03 - 12:04 - 12:05 - 12:06 - 12:07 - 12:08 - 12:09 - 12:10 - 12:11 - 12:12 - 12:13 - 12:14 - 12:15 - 12:16 - 12:17 - 12:18 - 12:19 - 12:20 - 12:21 - 12:22 - 12:23 - 12:24 - 12:25 - 12:26 - 12:27 - 12:28

- 12:29 - 12:30 - 12:31- 12:32 - 12:33 - 12:34 - 12:35 - 12:36 - 12:37 - 12:38 - 12:39 - 12:40 - 12:41.

Lying on the grassy slope above the pond at Pinafore Park. Afternoon clouds starting to gather. Charlie and me figuring what are the odds of finding some work to go along-side our railroad jobs. Me a brakeman, way down on the totem pole of guys they call in when they got some work. Charlie a fireman, and he hasn't had more than two or three days a month when somebody calls in sick. Well look – It's June, and I heard that they're going to have a good harvest this year out West. They're gonna need an awful lot of farm hands to bring her all in. They don't have those harvest trains any more. You gotta get there on your own. So – a dollar a day and work every day, what with all those farmers crying for help? I'm saying why don't we go on the hobo and ride out there on the trains?

Left St. Thomas at 2:10 am. Rode way-car to Toronto. had breakfast with trainmen.

"The earth is often thought of as an oblate spheroid as it has been observed that it is flattened at the poles."

He is lying on his back. He can't tell where he is. In the sunshine on the grassy slope at the park? In his mother's house, at home? In a ditch beside a railroad track? In a boxcar? In a barn? In a jail? There is a great weight on his chest. It feels like a massive stone, but he can't lift his arms so he cannot touch it. The stone presses down on his chest. He hears the walls closing in, but he cannot see them. It is dark so all he has are his ears and his thoughts. How long have I been lying here in the dark?

"Many Canadians are riding the rails in search of work."

The way things are going - what are the odds - a good harvest - get there on your own - an oblate spheroid - its axis of rotation - can't tell where he is - a great weight - the stone presses down - the walls closing in.

Well, both my parents came from England. My mother came from up North and my dad came from somewhere else, but I don't know where. They lived in Poplar, I think, before they came out here.

My grandparents stayed back in England, so I never knew them at all. My mother's father was a very old man, like Father Christmas, with a big white beard. There's a picture of him with my older sister when she was knee-high.

I don't really know a lot about England. That's where all our people are from. There wasn't much there for my parents, so they came out here.

Cyril Passfield: Out West

Life is long
said the boy
to the old man.

I know a guy with a section of land in Vermillion. Len Yarwood – remember we worked with him on the Anderson farm? Len's way far up in northern Alberta. We could go up there and get some work with him. Even if he's got enough help for himself, he'll be sure to know someone else who could use a few good hands. And both of us know horses. We're the kind they need out there. These guys from Toronto have never had a blister on their hands. We could work there for a while and then move on to the coast. Must be freighters from there going out all over the world.

Rested in park all day. entertained by Hungarians dancing. Slept in boxcar in yards; had hazardous time getting out of W. Toronto.

"It has always been a challenge for cartographers to represent the spherical earth on the flat surface that a map presents to the eye."

Swimming at the pond.
Wondering what to do.

She sits on the verandah with her two youngest sons. "Charlie knows a guy out West. A guy who worked with us on the Anderson farm when he was here. It's not as if we're going into this blind. I'll write as soon as we get there. I'll send you an address. I'm sorry about that fence. Hate to promise something and then not do what I say. Told the railroad I'd be gone for the summer. Start back in when I return. It'll be the same for Charlie. Hey look, I can't sit around here and watch you cooking meals for those people and all you let me do to help is to stir the pot. Me and Charlie'll be making a dollar a day and every day there'll be work for us to do. They say the harvest is going to be good this year, so we'll have our choice of farms. We'll be back at the end of the summer with our pockets full of cash. If this Depression lets up there'll be more work for us here in the fall." She hears the crunch of boots on the gravel drive. Her youngest son will drive the two boys to the train.

It is dark - from somewhere else - I don't really know - wasn't much there - be sure to know - the kind they need - all over the world - had hazardous time - may be defined - going into this blind.

So my dad came to Poplar from some other English city. My mother told me one time but I don't know which one. He was a plasterer, worked on the docks, and ran a store.

He was a pretty all-round person. Shipwright, carpenter, bricklayer – plasterer too. Brought all his tools when he came out to Canada.

He was good with music and wood. Sharpening a saw or playing the concertina. Always working around the house or playing a tune.

Pluck the grapes
one by one
said the poet.

Packing everything Charlie and me thinks we're gonna need. The little pack I always take when we go to Detroit. Good idea to take our railroad duds for when we're walking though the yards. Those bulls they have in those yards are tough as nails. Change of shirt and socks and underwear. Razor and bar of soap. Camera and a couple rolls of film. Twenty-five dollars each and leave the rest at home. The whole thing rolled up in a blanket that fits on our back.

A woman on her knees scrubbing floors.
A boy reading a book in a barn.
A fortuneteller opening a door.

Sunday June 19 1932 - Monday June 20 1932 - Tuesday June 21 1932 - Wednesday June 22 1932 - Thursday June 23 1932 - Friday June 24 1932 - Saturday June 25 1932.

What is Oak Street?
What is St. Thomas?
What is Ontario?

"Once upon a time a baby was born on a small street in a small town in a big country."

St. Thomas - Ingersoll - Woodstock - Drumbo - Galt - Puslinch - Toronto - Bolton - Beston - Essa - Medonte - Bala - McTier - Shawabaga - Point Au Baril - Wanikewan - Worthington - Wanup - Romford - Sudbury.

A family listening to hockey on the radio.
A railroad diamond with dozens of tracks.
Two girls skipping rope on a sidewalk.

Leaving St. Thomas in the dark. Two-ten a.m. on June nineteenth. Riding the way-car heading for Toronto. Watching the scenery from the caboose. All the farms as dark as can be. Just the odd lantern in a barn here and there. A sliver of moon behind the clouds. The only lights are in the towns. The railroad guys making breakfast of bacon and toast. Stopping at every station.

Dropping off news and taking on milk. Sipping coffee and stretching our legs and thinking of what we're gonna do when we get out West. Planning to wear our railroad overalls every time we come to the yards. We can walk right past the police as they make their arrests. Won't be able to tell us from the guys who work on the trains. We don't even look like hoboes when we wear our duds.

Jumped an empty, rode all day on a local. helped trainmen unload merchandise. Rode waycars often, in the North Country.

"The word 'weather' refers to localized atmospheric conditions which change on a daily basis."

"Hobo jungles are filled with the wandering unemployed."

She fills the vase with water and places it on the counter next to the sink. Don't worry about me, I told him. I've always been all right. I've got plenty to keep me busy. No fear of that. She picks up a rose and gives the stem a snip with the scissors. Another rose – another snip. Three in all. Then she places them in the water in the vase. The clock is ticking on the mantle. Begin at ten, dinner at eight. Plenty of time to cook and serve. They were very pleased when I catered their last affair. Four months – from June to October. He told me not to worry. Said the crops are good this year. He and his friend will be back in St. Thomas in no time at all. She puts the vase on the table on the verandah. Don't bother telling me not to worry. There's no sense in worrying. Worrying's the thing that never gets you anywhere.

To work with horses - the fort was surrounded - a secret tunnel - smorgasbord of food - important part of the universe - a very small unit - beyond conception - about right for me - swept it away.

My mother came from Egremont, Cumberland. She said the kids all used to play on the slag heaps. A mining town.

Right up on the Scottish border. Her father worked with horses. I've always liked to work with horses too.

She said they had a fort that was centuries old. And if the fort was surrounded, they had a secret tunnel. That tunnel would lead you way back out on the moors.

Climb the hill
path or not
to the top.

A street in Toronto. Walking along with a couple of hoboes. Must look like we are too. Anybody looking at us would think we're a couple of them. A block of streets at the edge of the yards. Checking the alleys for thrown-away food. Just look it over for maggots before you chow down! Bread is always good. They throw it out when it's too stale to sell. Any vegetables always go good in a pot of stew. Then back to the railroad yards. Hungarians dancing beside a big fire. One guy on a fiddle and most of them clapping their hands. A great big smorgasbord of food. Everything we got from the stores in a cauldron. Singing and dancing far into the night. We should crawl into one of these boxcars and get some sleep.

Saw Coppercliff mine at Sudbury. 7 miles of track underground. Gigantic chimney there. 527 feet high. 40' base. 16 feet in diameter at the top.

"Neither the size nor the shape of the universe is known to we who live on the earth."

He rubs his hands and leans closer to the fire. He is sitting beside the young fellow on the ground. The pieces of kindling he gathered up are coming to life. "Everything I had was just about right for me. Then this whole thing came along and swept it away. Don't think I'll travel far any more. Just stick around here and take it day by day." Others come and dump their scroungings on the fire. "These are terrible times, but they can't go on forever. All these fellows want is a job and couple of dollars in their hands." More and more join the scrum as the fire gets warm. "Long ways to go between here and the coast." The pine branches crackle and the logs begin to sizzle as the water in them boils. He pulls the diary from his pocket as he talks. "You're going to see a lot more than you do. Don't let things go by without you. Look around and see what there is to see. A lot of tears; a lot of smiles. But don't forget you're part of it too. Make sure you get your own place near the fire."

Taking a waycar to Toronto.
Hopping a freight train heading north.

Terrible times - long ways to go - look around and see - your own place - notice everything - just startin' out - the other end - two or three roses - leave the thorns - off to see the world.

And then when my mother got older she got a job in London. A housemaid in those swanky houses they have. And my dad's sister was working there as well.

My dad's sister was the cook in this big old house. And she said, "I have a brother who'd be just right for you." And she introduced them and that's how the two of them met.

So my parents got married and set up a store in Poplar. A greengrocer shop near London. Right down where the ships all dock.

*The waters meet
the waters part
where you stand.*

This old fellow giving me a diary and a stubby little pencil. While we're sitting in the hobo jungle down in the yards. Write down everything you see. Everything you hear. Don't let nothin' get away from you, he says. Whatever takes your attention. That's the way to ride the rails. Notice everything and jot down a word or two. I picked you out when you first set down beside the fire. Seen the way you handled yourself. You let them other fellows talk and you listened in. You and your friend are just startin' out. I'm at the other end of the trail. You looked like the kind of young man I should give this diary to.

12:00 - 12:01 - 12:02 - 12:03 - 12:04 - 12:05 - 12:06 - 12:07 - 12:08 - 12:09 - 12:10 - 12:11 - 12:12 - 12:13 - 12:14 - 12:15 - 12:16 - 12:17 - 12:18 - 12:19 - 12:20 - 12:21 - 12:22 - 12:23 - 12:24 - 12:25 - 12:26 - 12:27 - 12:28 - 12:29 - 12:30 - 12:31 - 12:32 - 12:33 - 12:34 - 12:35 - 12:36 - 12:37 - 12:38 - 12:39 - 12:40 - 12:41.

*The roses
on the trellis
are out in bloom.*

*A family carefully posing for a photograph.
A sleeper with a weight on his chest.
The grain in a piece of white oak.*

*Go and get mommy
two or three roses
for the vase.*

What are your thoughts?
What are your feelings?
What are your plans?

*Just the roses
mind you –
leave the thorns.*

Hopping a freight at the top of the yards. Lots of railroad police around. They carry those rubber truncheons and swing 'em hard. Charlie and me sneaking between the boxcars. Racing to an empty and scrambling inside.

Finally she starts to move. Picking up speed as she rolls along. Nice to see the fields go by. Farmland giving way to rock. Heading north out of Toronto. On our way right across Canada – Northern Ontario, Manitoba, Saskatchewan, Alberta and BC. Me and Charlie huddling down. Collars up for the cold morning air. Have to shout to make each other hear. We'll go right on out to the coast! Sleep on a bench in Stanley Park! Hop a freighter and we'll be off to see the world!

Chapter 2

Wandering through the yards at MacTier. Not sure which tracks to follow. Wanting to hop a freight but which way to go? Asking a trainman if he'll sell us a loaf of bread. Says he won't take anything for it and where are we headed? You're trainmen? You work on the roads? Why didn't you say so? A brakeman and a fireman! You should be wearin' your overalls so people can tell! You're headin' all the way out to the coast? You an' everybody else! Come on inside the caboose and I'll make you a meal! Gimme back that loaf of bread and come on inside!

Explained the country.

Flapjacks sizzling on an iron grill.
Railroad police with rubber-soled shoes.
A man carefully crafting a leather harness.

Bought a watch.

A lady and her daughter making sandwiches.
A truck with blocks of ice on the back.
A boy pouring syrup on his pancakes.

Started out to walk.

What are you noticing as you travel?
What are the things that you want to know?
Is there anything important enough to write down?

12:42 - 12:43 - 12:44 - 12:45 - 12:46 - 12:47 - 12:48 - 12:49 - 12:50 - 12:51- 12:52 - 12:53 - 12:54 - 12:55 - 12:56 - 12:57 - 12:58 - 12:59 - 1:00 - 1:01 - 1:02 - 1:03 - 1:04 - 1:05 - 1:06 - 1:07 - 1:08 - 1:09 - 1:10 - 1:11 - 1:12

- 1:13 - 1:14 - 1:15 - 1:16 - 1:17 - 1:18 - 1:19 - 1:20 - 1:21 - 1:22 - 1:23 - 1:24.

Raining a little out of Sudbury. Riding along inside the cupola of caboose. Couldn't be having a nicer ride in a limousine. Sitting on chairs at the back of the caboose as the brakeman explains the country. Beautiful country up here. Largely rocks and trees. Coppercliff mine with gigantic chimneys. A warning about the conductor. Don't know him very well. A new man, as far as I'm concerned. Might insist we follow the rules. If he says you're off why then you'll both have to go. The conductor coming in through the door. Great big guy with a bushy red beard. Eyes as fierce as a mad dog. The brakeman explaining to him who we are. Two railway boys from St. Thomas, on their way to the coast. Shaking our hands and telling us both of youse sit right back down.

Rained a little out of Sudbury. We rode in the cupola, and the Condr. + Brk. explained the country to us. Largely rocks and trees.

"A glance at a globe will show that the earth may be considered as having two surfaces – that of water and that of land."

Two calves in the pen. He leans against the fence and looks at the calves. It had been out of sheer frustration. These calves are worth, I would guess, five dollars each. They'll be gone next year and I'll have nothing left to show. The binder was worth a whole lot more than that.

"The economy has been sliding downward since the summer of 1929."

Which way to go - come on inside - explains the country - a warning - follow the rules - fierce as a mad dog - rather amorphous term - any configuration - not visibly covered - a cheaper ticket.

I don't know why my parents came to Canada. I guess the greengrocer shop had failed. Canada was a cheaper ticket than Australia, so they came out here.

Both my parents had great big families in England. Brothers and sisters and parents too. They used to write back and forth when they first came out.

Used to be a big bundle of letters in the attic. I never read them 'cause the people aren't real to me. After my dad died, none of his family wrote letters at all.

Who will pull the donkey cart
now the donkey's dead?

Huddling under a tarpaulin. Nothing to eat since yesterday in Kenora. Having to shout to talk at all. Never seen rain come down as hard as this back home! Those cops looked pretty mean! That was pretty dangerous stuff! She was goin' pretty fast when we jumped on! Rain and sleet slashing at the canvas. A rope comes loose and we make a few grabs at the flapping canvas and tie it down. Thunder crashing and lightning ripping across the sky. Shouting once in a while. I get the idea we're on the main line! Won't be too bad when this rain settles down! Hope it's the Winnipeg express! If we're right this train should take us all the way!

Arrived in Winnipeg. Had a shower, bought a watch and called up some friends. Where we were invited out to dinner next day.

"It must be kept in mind that any attempt to present a spherical object on a flat surface must inevitably lead to a certain amount of distortion."

Riding inside the trains.
Huddling on the flatcars.

He sits on the platform. Weaving finger-rings. Intricate. Exquisite. Sublime. Hundreds of people come and go. Every one of them is broke – not a dime.

Pull the donkey cart - the people aren't real - great big families - pretty dangerous stuff - on the main line - without some distortion - intricate, exquisite, sublime - to check the bills - won't take a single dime - the little girl died.

My sister, Margaret, was born in England. She must have lived there about seven years. They brought her out to Canada when they came out here.

She works in a bank in Detroit. Worked as a waitress in St. Thomas, but got laid off. Went over to Detroit with my brother, Bob, to try to find work.

She showed us how to check the bills for counterfeit. Closes her eyes and runs her fingers over the bills. She can only do it with American dollar bills.

A vase fell off the mantelpiece and broke.
There didn't seem to be a reason why it fell.

Winnipeg. Cold and wet and tired. Directed from the yards to the Salvation Army Hotel. Hot water and a home-cooked meal. Friendly advice and a clean, warm bed. Tired and cold and soaking wet. Needing a bath and a shave and a meal. We've gotta pay these people for the privilege. We were willing to take a hotel. It's not as if we're broke like everyone else. In the morning we offer him money. About half what we figured to pay somewhere else. A frown on his face. A scowl as he raises his hand and waves us away. We insist, but he tells us he won't take a single dime.

Two colts cavorting like puppies in a field.
The fingers worn out of leather gloves.
Vegetables bubbling in a pot of hobo stew.

Sunday June 26 1932 - Monday June 27 1932 - Tuesday June 28 1932 - Wednesday June 29 1932 - Thursday June 30 1932 - Friday July 1 1932.

Why do people always say that things will get better?
Why are they willing to put their shoulders to the wheel?
Do they look around to see who's holding the whip?

"The boy was a twin when he was born but that didn't last too long as the little girl died within a month of her birth."

Cartier - Pogamising - Metagama - Bistcotasing - Ramsay - Woman River - Kinogama - Chapleau - Wayland - Dalton - Missanabie - Franz - Grasset - Amyot - White River - Brenner - Struthers - Heron Bay - Middleton - Jack Fish Bay.

A padlock on a chain-link fence.
Work camps offering twenty cents a day.
A woman lifting her child onto a boxcar.

Sitting in a restaurant on the edge of the Winnipeg yards. Now what can we afford? Both of us ordering the same. Sipping our coffee as we wait. A little stingy with the refills and not much talk. Finally, the two plates come. There's a crack in one of the plates. A pork chop encased in batter. Sticking a fork in and something yellow starts oozing out! What in the heck is this! We shoulda ordered the omelet! Calling the lady over to explain. She doesn't bring the coffee pot. What's this yellow matter oozing out of this thing? That's butter, she says and turns and walks away.

Had a shower and started out to walk to Portage La Prairie. Very tiresome walking. Found a bottle of beer, got a few rides. Tried to board a train out of Portage and the cop chased us off. Waited all day, and got one out at night. Arrived in Brandon and had a shower at the Y.

"A meteorologist is a person who applies scientific principles to the collection and analysis of weather data with the objective of predicting future weather patterns."

"Many farmers are in arrears with their property taxes and facing foreclosure."

Seven people sit around the dinner table. It is Sunday so they are all in fancy clothes. The father wears a tie and a waistcoat. The mother a white blouse and a skirt. The girls and boys in their blouses and their ties.

Not much talk - what in the heck - turns and walks away - the exacting science - the prediction of the future - application of scientific principles - around the dinner table - came from somewhere - a grasshopper plague - you can't even see.

My brother, Bob, was born in England. He quit school when our father died. Fourteen years old and out to work.
An apprentice on the railroad. Then off to Detroit to learn a trade. Drafting, mechanical drawing – studied at nights.
Now he's designing parts of automobiles. Works in an office on Washington Boulevard. Building a house in Mt. Clemens, near Detroit, for him and his wife and their son.

Your parents came from somewhere
over the sea
far away.

Walking to Portage la Prairie. Eighty miles with no hope of a ride in sight. A grasshopper plague all through the countryside. Flying up in clouds as we walk along the highway. Don't seem to be any houses around. Somebody must own these fields. Will anything be left of the crops when these things have their fill? Wonder if the farms have been abandoned. Grasshoppers so thick that you can't even see the crops!

Saw the sights of Brandon. Had dinner and left that afternoon for Moose Jaw. Passed through the city of Regina Sun. night, and eluded the cops, who were wearing rubber soled shoes.

"We use the word 'universe' to encompass everything that is to be found in the earth and in the heavens beyond."

Climbing up Sulphur Mountain. Altitude seven thousand four hundred and ninety feet above sea-level. Having a heck of a time. A long way, but both boys are game. Their feet keep slipping and sliding on the loose shale. One of them grabs at an outcrop of rock and it gives way and tumbles down and misses the other boy by a fraction of an inch. Every once in a while they pause and exchange the lead. Neither one of them ever thinks of going back down.

Walking miles and miles.
Seeking out the shade.

Eluded the cops - the whole of space - heck of a time - a fraction of an inch - plenty of water - looks and tastes and smells - gulping handfuls down - a trickle of water - a loaf of bread - can't even eat.

My sister, Hilda, is older than me. About eight years older, I think. She was born in England too.

She works at Alma College. One of the maids. That's a girls' school where young ladies come to be refined.

She's been there since she was fifteen. Six days a week with room and board. Meets our mother at church on Sundays and walks with her home.

Took a course in basketry. She makes things for the house. Fern stands, flower vases – things like that.

He always sleeps so soundly.
Exhausted by work or by play.
Every day drains the sap that night restores.

Forgot to bring along something to drink. Thought we'd be finding lots of creeks along the way. Getting parched as we walk along. Finally a little old shack, set off a ways from the road. A woman answering the door. Big rough lady with a child on her hip. Saying we'll do some work if she'll kindly give us a drink. Plenty of water in the well, she says, but her husband just put in new cribbing and the water might still be tasting of brand-new wood. Sniffing and tasting a handful of water. Looks and tastes and smells all right. Agreeing to take the chance. Both of our throats are pretty dry. Gulping handfuls down and finally slaking our thirst.

12:42 - 12:43 - 12:44 - 12:45 - 12:46 - 12:47 - 12:48 - 12:49 - 12:50 - 12:51- 12:52 - 12:53 - 12:54 - 12:55 - 12:56 - 12:57 - 12:58 - 12:59 - 1:00 - 1:01 - 1:02 - 1:03 - 1:04 - 1:05 - 1:06 - 1:07 - 1:08 - 1:09 - 1:10 - 1:11 - 1:12 - 1:13 - 1:14 - 1:15 - 1:16 - 1:17 - 1:18 - 1:19 - 1:20 - 1:21 - 1:22 - 1:23 - 1:24.

A family
posing
for a photograph.

Horses turning away from the dirt in the wind.
Hot water and a home-cooked meal.
A widow reading letters from her son.

*Standing
in front of their house
in the garden.*

Would you say that your society has failed you?
Does it owe you something more than it has paid?
Is there a better life for you somewhere else?

*It's spring
and all the flowers
are in bloom.*

Taking a break in a stand of trees. A can of meat and a loaf of bread. A trickle of water fresh as can be. Charlie taking out his knife to cut the bread. This bread is like a rock! We cut all that firewood for a loaf of bread and now we can't even eat it! She shoulda told us to bring the axe! Charlie hacking away for a while and then tearing off a few chunks and sprinkling them with water from the stream. A little soggy, but we dine on meat and bread.

Chapter 3

Walking into Portage La Prairie. Ten o'clock at night. Everything closed up tight as a drum. Where in the heck are we going to eat? Where will we stay? Talking to a cop on the corner. Spend the night in the jail if you want to. Will they let us out in the morning? You bet they will. Put you out and on the road. Treat you like kings in the meantime, though. Give you a cell and a bed and a mattress. Nice warm blanket to keep off the cold. Six o'clock wake-up call in the morning. Give you a chit to go and have breakfast. Only one restaurant in town. Hope you guys like Chinese.

On the wrong train.

Swimmers floating on the surface of the water.
A bullwhip snapping a cigarette.
A packsack on a bunk in a jail.

Washed up in the jungle.

A family riding in a horse-drawn automobile.
Knee-high grass growing through a rusty plough.
A limousine with a for-sale sign on the windshield.

Mounties on guard.

Is there agony in the kingdom?
Are the peasants not content?
Has the economic crisis cast a pall?

1:25 - 1:26 - 1:27 - 1:28 - 1:29 - 1:30 - 1:31- 1:32 - 1:33 - 1:34 - 1:35 - 1:36 - 1:37 - 1:38 - 1:39 - 1:40 - 1:41- 1:42 - 1:43 - 1:44 - 1:45 - 1:46 - 1:47 - 1:48 - 1:49 - 1:50 - 1:51- 1:52 - 1:53 - 1:54 - 1:55 - 1:56 - 1:57 - 1:58 - 1:59 - 2:00 - 2:01 - 2:02 - 2:03 - 2:04 - 2:05 - 2:06.

A man playing a mouth organ. Sitting on the edge of the platform at the end of the railroad station. Trains coming in and trains going out. Nothing to do and nowhere to go. Porters with packages. Agents with clipboards. Two or three hobos waiting for trains. How can all these trains be going in the same direction? We're lookin' to go East! We already been out West! Seems like every one of these here trains is goin' the wrong way! The guy on the mouth organ keeps on playing. He doesn't look East and he doesn't look West. Never heard that tune he's playing. Hard to even call it a tune. Just a bunch of notes that he's trying to make into a tune. He plays so slow it's like he'll be playing those notes all day.

Arrived in Moose Jaw at 3 am. The Moose Jaw yards is one of the biggest on the continent.

"The term 'sky' is, like 'sunrise' and 'sunset', an amorphous term which is avoided by serious scientists."

Two Studebakers in the shed. One with a broken axle and one that works. The gas can bumps against the post as he moves between them. He has a roll of rubber hose in his pocket. He removes the cap from the filler-pipe of the gasoline tank. I've come to think we all went loco in '25.

"Since 1929, the Gross National Product has fallen by forty-two percent."

A nice warm blanket - everything closes - put you out - give you a cell - give you a chit - sitting on the edge - nothing to do - nowhere to go - goin' the wrong way - never heard that tune.

So Ken is my younger brother. He's a cutter at Nursery Shoe. Cuts leather out for the shoes and all like that.
Ken was only a boy when Dad died. So it had no effect on him. We never talk about our dad at all.
I left Ken with the keys to my car. A 1927 Chev. Makes it easier for Mom with someone who knows how to drive.

Chances are
your future
will be sunshine.

Sleeping in boxcars, on the ground, in train stations and in jails. On locomotives, in the caboose and on cars of coal. Talking to the trainmen about our jobs. How Eastern trains are different than Western trains. Brakemen, switchmen, oilers, conductors. Telling them carpentry work is my favourite.

Fixing everything made of wood in the stations and yards. A brotherhood of trainmen. Being invited into the cabooses. Many insisting we sleep in their beds. Cooking us meals and giving us tickets to ride on the trains.

Got on the wrong train and eventually started right for Medicine Hat. (Lights on all year. Natural gas.) Big ranch country, rather dry, much sage brush. Saw and heard many rattlesnakes Also saw cowboys, and herds of cattle.

"The best that can be done under the circumstances is to attempt to reduce the amount of distortion to acceptable proportions.

Waiting for a train.
Sleeping on the ground.

Madame Florina is about to lock the door. Now where did I put my glasses? She concentrates as she fumbles with the lock. She has a stricken look on her face.

A bunch of notes - has given way - all went loco - precise and useful terms - had no effect - chances are - fixing everything - giving us tickets - on the wrong train - it is the objective.

I was a twin when I was born. A girl who died right away. In those days, the funerals would start out at the house.
Dorothy Lillian Passfield. Three months old when she died. My oldest sister said she was very weak at birth.
Hard to think of her as a person. Would have been just as old as me. Same years, hours and minutes – same number of beats as my heart.

The tree was very deep in the forest.
Half in sunlight; half in shade.
An ancient oak whose trunk was gnarled and scarred.

A lesson in how to stem. Stemming is the art of asking for food. Always offer to do some jobs around the house. Nobody likes to beg, but it isn't really begging, you see. It's offering to work in exchange for food. None of these people is rich but they try to help. Some got sons on the bum, you know, who are just like us. Most people want firewood chopped, or maybe a fence needs a little repair or something like that. One guy wanted his septic tank cleaned but I told the guy no thanks. Sandwiches are the best. You can take 'em back to the yards. Whatever you get you can share with the other guys. When we pool what we get we all have a hobo feast.

The death of a family donkey.
A figure moving towards a barn in the dark.
Two sleepers on the floor of a boxcar.

Saturday July 2 1932 - Sunday July 3 1932 - Monday July 4 1932 - Tuesday July 5 1932 - Wednesday July 6 1932 - Thursday July 7 1932 - Friday July 8 1932.

Are people born to live in luxury?
Are they born to pull a cart?
Is there any kind of plan to this at all?

"The boy had a father and a mother and an older brother and two older sisters and a younger brother and they all lived in a house at the end of the street."

Schreiber - Rossport - Dublin - Nipigon - Pearl - Loon - Port Arthur - Fort William - Kaminisigula - Buda - Raith - Upsala - Niblock - Bonheur - Ignace - Raleigh - Dryden - Eagle River - Vermillion Bay - Pine.

A stack of firewood beside a house.
A man trading a dime for a newspaper.
A woman scrubbing clothes on a washboard.

A farmhouse near Swift Current. She starts to set the table. I say I haven't got much time. I only wanted sandwiches. I'd be glad to chop some wood. No – she wants to cook me a meal. Doesn't need any firewood for now. Just sit and relax and the kettle be boilin' soon. But the fellows back at the yard are waiting for me. Only take a little while, she says. You must be tired from all that travellin'. Got nice cups here in the cupboard. These here plates are my Sunday-best. I pick these flowers fresh every day that I put in the vase. You just set back and rest your feet. You said your feet was sore. Got the kettle already on. Be boilin' soon.

Arrived in Medicine Hat in the afternoon, and washed up in the river. Our mate "stemmed" a lunch and we ate in the park. Caught a double header pulling up the hill and rode a flat car to Calgary. Washed up in the jungle at the river.

"*The meteorologist begins his predictions by plotting weather data on a huge map of the area with which he is concerned.*"

"Thousands of Canadians are in danger of starving or freezing to death."

A father and his boy. Walking along hand in hand. They pause and look both ways as they cross the street. The father carries a box. It is round with flattened sides. It hangs from a leather strap by his side.

To utilize methods - distortion can be reduced - fumbles with the lock - has a stricken look - very weak at birth - half in sunlight - half in dark - same number of beats - whatever you get - pool what we get.

My dad died when I was seven. I don't remember much about him. What you don't remember you can't really think about.

I never asked my mother what he was like. She never wanted to talk about my dad. She was too busy making things right for the kids.

The first I remember, my dad was on the railroad. It don't remember him working at anything else. Worked as a carpenter in the shop.

A little gnome in a little red hat at the foot of the garden.
A group of people were looking for Jimmy's little red ball.

Three of us in a boxcar. Charlie and me and the guy who taught us how to stem. Overalls rolled up as a pillow. Slight breeze coming in through the door. Clicking rails and drifting off to sleep. Awoken with a shake! Looking around to see what's wrong! Pretty deep asleep when I get the nudge. Charlie's pretty upset. Caught this guy going through your pack! I watched him and he searched it pretty good! The fellow backing towards the door. Scrambling up to my feet. I was just lookin' for a match! That's all I was doin'! We kick his pack towards him and Charlie says, You're out! The train is chugging up a grade. He grabs his pack and turns and jumps on out the door. Didn't notice, I guess, that neither one of us smokes.

Stayed overnight in Calgary, left for B. C. 3 PM. Arrived in Banff at night. Mounties on guard, looked over train. Went to sleep on car of autoes. took pictures from train. Thru Field at midnight. Connaught tunnel – 5 miles long.

"The early peoples assumed, quite naturally for them, that the earth was the centre of all creation."

The screen door slaps shut and he walks across the porch and across the yard and leans on the fence. The two young colts cavort like puppies. He loves to watch them after work if the gang gets back in daylight. Born this spring and feeling frisky. He walks to the barn and scoops up a handful of oats. He has them eating out of his hand in no time at all.

Offering work for food.
Washing in a river.

Round with flattened sides - don't remember much - foot of the garden - people were looking - get the nudge - people of ancient times - centre of this universe - hardly breaking the surface - gotta show you something - two of us scrambling.

On Sundays, my dad would go 'round and read for people. A lot of old people don't know how to read. Read their letters and write out replies and things like that.
And I'd go with him and they would give me tea and a biscuit. And he used to play the accordion and the organ and the piano. He'd sit at night by the fire and play the concertina – all those old English songs that people knew.
And he'd play at different gatherings. People didn't have any money, but they were always getting together. Weddings and other affairs like my mother caters to now.

At night the puppet became the puppeteer.

Medicine Hat in the afternoon. Washing up in the river. Stemming a lunch and eating in the park. Hopping a flatcar for a ride to Calgary. Washing up beneath a bridge on some gravel flats. Deciding to take a swim. Charlie diving off a rock and right back out! Only in the water for a second! Hardly breaking the surface at all! Shivering like he's in the Arctic! Never felt water as cold as that! Must be coming right off of a glacier and into this park!

1:25 - 1:26 - 1:27 - 1:28 - 1:29 - 1:30 - 1:31 - 1:32 - 1:33 - 1:34 - 1:35 - 1:36 - 1:37 - 1:38 - 1:39 - 1:40 - 1:41- 1:42 - 1:43 - 1:44 - 1:45 - 1:46 - 1:47 - 1:48 - 1:49 - 1:50 - 1:51- 1:52 - 1:53 - 1:54 - 1:55 - 1:56 - 1:57 - 1:58 - 1:59 - 2:00 - 2:01 - 2:02 - 2:03 - 2:04 - 2:05 - 2:06.

The lettuce
glistens brightly
in the sunshine.

Books of wisdom sitting on a shelf.
A train-wreck at the bottom of a gulch.
The lobby of an eleven-story hotel.

The leaves
plump up
with the morning rain.

A drop of rain at the top of a mountain?
A piece of wreckage at the bottom of a gorge?
What do you see as your rightful place in the world?

The roots
put down
an anchor in the soil.

Riding through the mountains. Kicking Horse Pass. Big oil-burning locomotive. The engineer and the fireman giving us a ride. Come back with me, says the fireman. I just gotta show you somethin'. You can see it better from a flatcar two or three back. Three of us climbing over the coal. Sitting on the edge of a flatcar with our feet dangling over the canyon. A long way down but we're only going ten miles an hour. Sun and a bit of a breeze as we're chugging along. Now look up here as we pass this bluff, the fireman says. We look up and my god it's a grizzly bear! Head and paws hanging over the rock, looking down at us! Big head and all tongue and teeth! Our feet dangling over the canyon! A mile or two straight down! And a grizzly bear looking to have us both for lunch! The fireman laughing his head off! The two of us scrambling back to the middle of the car!

Chapter 4

Charlie calling out to me to come on over here! We sling our packs inside and climb aboard. Settling down inside a grain car. The choice of all the boxcars in the yards. All lined with heavy brown paper. The grain all emptied out and the paper still here. We've been sleeping in ditches and barns. Freezing in empty boxcars and dodging the rains. Roll the overalls up as a pillow. Spread your blanket out on the floor. Pull a sheet of the heavy brown paper over top of you. Warmer than the blankets we brought from home. We could wake up covered in frost and be as warm as toast inside. The perfect way to sleep as a hobo. Neither of us can believe our luck. Smelling the odour of the wheat as I drift on off to sleep.

Awoke nearly frozen.

A carpentering job on the railroad.
A walk of fourteen miles.
A singsong around a piano.

Hit a section man.

A crowd lining the block at a movie theatre.
People dancing at a wedding in a hall.
Salmon jumping up a mountain spring.

Very cosmopolitan city.

Would you rather be living in England?
Would your father still be alive?
Family gatherings for feasts at holiday times?

2:07 - 2:08 -2:09 - 2:10 - 2:11 - 2:12 - 2:13 - 2:14 - 2:15 - 2:16 - 2:17 - 2:18 - 2:19 - 2:20 - 2:21 - 2:22 - 2:23 - 2:24 - 2:25 - 2:26 - 2:27 - 2:28 - 2:29 - 2:30 - 2:31- 2:32 - 2:33 - 2:34 - 2:35 - 2:36 - 2:37 - 2:38 - 2:39 - 2:40

- 2:41- 2:42 - 2:43 - 2:44 - 2:45 - 2:46 - 2:47 - 2:48 - 2:49.

The train is covered with sleeping hoboes. All huddled on the tender to get some warmth. The brakeman inviting us in. C'mon inside! There's always room for railway men! Talking to him about our work on the railroads back home. Moving slowly through the mountains. Looking out the window of the cab. Look here! There's a bear on the track! A big old black bear and he looks like he's holdin' his ground! Aren't we going to stop? Naw, we can't be stoppin' for every bear that's on the tracks! The bear is intent on something. He doesn't make a move. Doesn't respond to the whistle-blowing. We hit him and he tumbles off the track. We both lean out the window and watch him tumbling over and over down the slope. Probably dead, but if he ain't, he'll be dead pretty soon! Broken leg or somethin' like that! Won't be able to hunt for food! Don't see how he can survive bein' hit by a train!

Awoke nearly frozen, speeding thru Kicking Horse Canyon. The brakeman invited us into the cab, as the tender was covered with sleeping Bo's. Killed a bear and hit a section man while riding on the cab of the oil burner.

"Although the term 'sea' is used indiscriminately by the amateur, more precise terms are used by professionals in reference to the many kinds of bodies of water which are found on the earth."

He sits at the kitchen table with a pencil and a piece of paper. A list of figures that don't seem to want to add up. His wife is doing the dishes. She puts a cup of tea down on the table, but he doesn't notice. Can't make these numbers work like I want them to.

"National income is only fifty-one percent of what it was in 1929."

Settling down inside - the choice of all - wake up covered in frost - the perfect way to sleep - believe our luck - the odour of wheat - hit a section man - room for railway men - a bear on the track - we can't be stoppin'.

And my dad was working in a boxcar one day. They used to wreck the old cars. And they put a big hook on the boxcar and heaved it down over a bank.
They were going to burn the boxcar. In those days all the boxcars were made of wood. He was salvaging the parts that could be saved.
So they heaved it over the bank. And the boxcar might have turned over once or twice. And my dad and this other guy were trapped inside.

The sun will pour down in streams of light.
More than I can believe.

Moving slowly through the mountains. About ten miles an hour. Talking with Charlie in the cab. A Section Gang of Chinese workers packing the rails. Suddenly we stop. The engineer puts on the brakes. Some guy fell and hit his head! Go down and have a look and let me know! We swing down and walk back with the fireman. Everybody in the gang is standing and looking down the slope. A guy is sitting there and holding onto a bush. Charlie and me go sliding down. His head is turned away. Are you hurt?, and he turns and he's spitting out his teeth! Blood all over his mouth as if his jaw has all been smashed. We call up to the foreman and he calls back, Ah, it's just a Chinaman! Calls this out to us right in front of the Chinese Section Gang. Well we can't just leave him here! All right! Put him in the caboose and we'll take him to the doctor! We help the man up the slope and clean his face as much as we can inside the caboose. A mummy wrapped in bloody handkerchiefs with tightly-closed eyes. Ten miles without a word from him and we help him off at a tiny station and get back on.

Arrived in Coquitlam, B.C. washed up in Fraser river. walked 8 miles towards Vancouver, were picked up by radio Cowboys from CFCX. had invitations to studio and dance.

"*A map, it must be considered, distorts the spherical globe that it represents in both area and shape.*"

Sleeping in a boxcar.
Helping a wounded man.

He sits there on the edge of the railway platform. He places his fingers on the holes of his whittled flute. Can't seem to find the tune. It's on the tips of my fingers. It's on the tip of my tongue. Can't play it, though, no matter how hard I try.

Tumbling over and over - awoke nearly frozen - a narrow definition - rules out much - a list of figures - make these numbers work - salvaging the parts - trapped inside - streams of light - more than I can believe.

He was inside and they put a big hook on and tipped her over and down she went. Down the bank, maybe fifteen feet. And they didn't know that he and this other fellow was inside.
So it shook him up pretty bad. And it caused an ulcer. So nobody knew that my father was bleeding inside.
And so they brought him home. And they put him on the verandah. And left my mother to nurse him back to health.

Look straight ahead at the house that you are building.
Do not look at the traffic passing by.

Washing up in the Frazer River. Walking at least eight miles in the rain. Hoping the sun will come out so we can dry off our packs. Picked up by radio cowboys. Squeezing us into the back of their car. Plenty of room for two more in here! Can't leave you out there in the rain! All the way from Ontario? How do you like it here in BC? Had enough rain to last you a lifetime? On their way to the radio station. Your dial should be rusted at CFCX! Singing radio jingles. Lonesome dogies and ridin' the range. Invitations to visit the studio and come to a dance. The wiper slaps the windshield as they sing.

A man striding across the grass.
A tree which trades in truth.
A puppet controlling the thoughts of a puppeteer.

Saturday July 9 1932 - Sunday July 10 1932 - Monday July 11 1932 - Tuesday July 12 1932 - Wednesday July 13 1932 - Thursday July 14 1932.

Would your grandparents still be living?
Would you have dozens of cousins as well?
How could your parents bear to leave their families behind?

"The boy's father worked on the railroad and his mother cleaned the house and cooked the meals and grew a garden and put up preserves against the winter."

Scovil - Kenora - Ingolf - Rennie - Whitemouth - Molson - East Selkirk - Winnipeg - Woodman - Rosser - Marquette - Rayburn - Portage La Prairie - MacGregor - Sydney - Camp Hughes - Chater - Brandon - Kennay - Griswold.

A flashlight searching in a boxcar.
A pile of dust covering most of a farm fence.
A man sleeping under a frost-covered blanket.

The hobo jungle in Vancouver. Going along with the gang to the markets to beg for food. Wilted lettuce and spoiled vegetables and whatever we can find. Hauling it all back to the jungle to make a stew. Take a knife and cut out the bad parts. Cooking it all in big pots. Groups of five or ten all gathered at different fires. Doctors, lawyers, teachers. Some in their battered, rumpled suits. Adjusting their ties each morning and scouring the city for work. No idea when this will be over. No idea where their families are now. If you sent some rent-money home, would they still be there?

VANCOVER. Raining, put in the day doging rains. ie museum and two shows. bought some souveniers, sent postcards.

"In the area of concern, there are weather stations which are designed to collect and record data which can be used to predict future weather-patterns."

"Alberta is in danger of defaulting on its debts."

The boy is sitting on the grass. He is looking down into a gully. There is a creek down below with a log across. It is the middle of the summer. The grass has dried from the morning rain. The sun is shining. It is late in the afternoon.

Invitations to visit - against the winter - cut out the bad parts - to observe and decode - the pain on his face - going to be all right - not seeking sea or land - won't be a burden - keep off the rain - proved wrong.

And he was all doubled over. You could see the pain on his face. And the sweat poured down and my mom would mop his brow.
And the doctor came out to see him. And he said, "Oh he's just got a cold. He's going to be all right in a few more days."
And my mother said to the doctor. "It's more than just a cold. This man is in agony – he can't straighten up."

Wisdom falls as rain falls,
not seeking sea nor land.

Women with kids around the fires. A little apart from all the men. Obviously travelling on their own. Trying to get someplace where they're able to feed their kids. How do these women expect to get kids on a boxcar? Old guys walking with a limp. Left home so they won't be a burden. How are they going to run alongside and jump a freight? Pretty tricky for Charlie and me. Slick footing from the rains. Engines picking up the speed. Yard police shouting and running towards you as you try to swing up on the cars. How do some of these people manage to stay alive?

Very cosmopolitan city, saw many turbaned Hindoos, and chinese coolies. Bamboo water wheels, dot the landscape. Chinese, in straw hats, corn husk coats to keep off the rain.

"It was only with the advent of the science of astronomy that humankind began to see the earth in relation to other heavenly bodies."

He mucked the barn out this morning and it's been drizzle the rest of the day. He drew from the well to water the cows. Ankle-deep puddles in the barnyard. He tried not to get drenched as he carried the pails. Now his back is against a comfortable pile of hay. *The earth is very nearly an oblate spheroid whose shorter axis coincides with its axis of rotation through the two poles.* Nice to have a day off, though he doesn't get paid. Reading from the *World Book* and thinking and reading again. Up in the loft with the door wide open and a view for miles.

    Singing radio jingles.
    Lining up for work.

A view for miles - thinking and reading - sepsis started to form - sower sows the seed - what he is and what he does - seventeen cents between us - could be anywheres - all over the world - anywhere there's water - ya gotta get a card.

And so the doctor left him at that. Just drove away in his car. And left my father dying there on the porch.

And then the abscess broke and they rushed him to the hospital. Put tubes in him and drained him for several days. But sepsis started to form and that finished him.

That left my mother alone with five children. She buckled right down and paid the bills. Cleaning people's houses and catering affairs.

    The sower sows the seed in the soil.
    What he is and what he does is his gift.

A bench in Stanley Park. People sleeping on newspapers on the grass. Four guys with a beat-up suitcase and a deck of cards. Rumours about jobs but no such thing when you track them down. Freighters hooting out in the harbour as they come and go. Me and Charlie holding out our hands. A dime in one, seven cents in the other. Seventeen cents between us. What'll we do? Think I should write a letter home? I could ask Ken to wire me some money. I left a twenty-dollar bill in my top drawer. In the box with the handkerchiefs I got last Christmas. A couple more days in this hobo jungle while we wait. Who was it told us there was jobs at the end of the line?

2:07 - 2:08 - 2:09 - 2:10 - 2:11 - 2:12 - 2:13 - 2:14 - 2:15 - 2:16 - 2:17 - 2:18 - 2:19 - 2:20 - 2:21 - 2:22 - 2:23 - 2:24 - 2:25 - 2:26 - 2:27 - 2:28 - 2:29 - 2:30 - 2:31 - 2:32 - 2:33 - 2:34 - 2:35 - 2:36 - 2:37 - 2:38 - 2:39 - 2:40 - 2:41 - 2:42 - 2:43 - 2:44 - 2:45 - 2:46 - 2:47 - 2:48 - 2:49.

*A young boy
running to meet
his dad.*

*Green and black marble sinks.
Circus workers playing cards in a cage.
The Hungarian words for food.*

*The father
putting
the lunch-box down.*

A miner like your ancestors?
Working with horses on a farm?
What would an English Cyril Passfield actually be?

*Swinging the boy
on his shoulders
for a ride.*

A grey July day in Vancouver. Seagulls circling over the bay. Lining up to apply for work on a freighter. Wonder where that one's going over there? Could be anywheres at all. There's ships from these docks goes out all over the world. Anywhere there's water – that's where they goes. There might be horses being shipped or maybe cattle. We could tend the stock while the sailors sail the ship. Wouldn't it be something for us to work our way to Hong Kong? Once in a while the whole line shuffles towards the shed. But ya gotta get a card, though. If you don't get no card, you ain't goin' nowhere. Only able-bodied seamen get to go. That shouldn't be so hard. With all these freighters in the docks, they must need hands. All these people coming out of the shed – are they all hired?

Chapter 5

Vancouver. Stanley Park again. Sleeping on a couple of benches under newspapers. Didn't like sending home for money. That wasn't the original idea at all. We came out here to make some ready cash. We better find some work soon or we'll be going home flat broke. We should have gone straight up to Vermillion. Did Len Yarwood say he had any work in that letter? Everyone says there's work out West, but just take a look around this park! There's hundreds of people get off the trains every day and end up here on these benches! All these guys line up every morning for one or two jobs!

An eerie ride.

A candle shining on a concertina.
Buffalo circling a rubbing stone.
Lining up to go to Hong Kong.

Witnessed three storms.

Railroad police with rubber-soled shoes.
A farm wagon filled with family furniture.
An employer announcing another cut in wages.

Nettles in my hand.

Put down stakes in British Columbia?
Live in Vancouver the rest of your life?
A Sunday stroll once a week in Stanley Park?

2:50 - 2:51 - 2:52 - 2:53 - 2:54 - 2:55 - 2:56 - 2:57 - 2:58 - 2:59 - 3:00 - 3:01 - 3:02 - 3:03 - 3:04 - 3:05 - 3:06 - 3:07 - 3:08 - 3:09 - 3:10 - 3:11 - 3:12 - 3:13 - 3:14 - 3:15 - 3:16 - 3:17 - 3:18 - 3:19 - 3:20 - 3:21 - 3:22 - 3:23 - 3:24 - 3:25 - 3:26 - 3:27 - 3:28 - 3:29 - 3:30 - 3:31.

Taking a bus to New Westminster. Sleeping in a boxcar overnight. Awaking to hear the trains pulling out of the yards. Chasing after one and catching it and swinging up inside. Riding all night through the countryside in a gentle rain. In the morning, people working on water wheels. The train comes lurching to a stop. Charlie and me both jumping down and having a feast. Raspberries! Wild raspberries! Growing all along the tracks! As big as the joints of our thumbs! The lurching train as we hop back on again.

Vancover. Woke up still raining. took bus to New Westminster. Had supper stayed in boxcar all night. Awoke to hear trains leaving yards, chased and caught it, and rode all night. A gentle rain kept us from sleeping further.

"The term 'earth' may be used in reference to any of the solid parts of the globe, hence it is a term which lends itself to many uses."

He had bought the binder new when times were good, but he had never been able to deal with its finicky ways. Then the rain had made it worse. He had nursed it along like a cripple all through the season. Jammed again when that light rain began to come down. The canvas straps had twisted and his nerves were at their ends.

"Industrial activity in Canada is now fifty-seven percent of what it was in 1925."

The original idea - one or two jobs - chasing after one - working on water wheels - having a feast - the inhabited terraqueous globe - nerves were at their ends - an eerie ride - may be correct - at the expense of the other.

He used to carry me on his shoulders. I used to meet him as he came up the hill. The roundhouse was over the gully from our house.
And he'd be carrying his lunch-pail. Left his carpentry tools at the shop. And he'd hoist me up on his shoulders and carry me home.
That's about all that I can remember. He was a very musical man. He came home every night as soon as the work was done.

Can we live without the donkey
now the donkey's dead?

Swaying boxcars in the rain. Making for an eerie ride. Through woods and out across bridges. Canyons looming down below. Rain pouring down in torrents. Lightning flashing across the sky. Occasional rays of moonlight showing log-booms down what seems like miles below. All the water in the heavens. Seems like it's gonna rain for months. Looking forward to riding the range in Alberta – couple of horses, herd of cattle, plenty of sun.

Rather an eerie ride, in the rain on the swaying boxcars. Thu woods lighted by flashes of lightening; across rivers, and waters lit by occasional rays of moon. Salmon canneries and log booms, looming large and fantastical.

"Cartographers can only make area or shape correct by allowing the distortion of the other element."

Sleeping on park benches.
Shivering in the rain.

Weaving rings to sell for money. All the rings arranged beside him on the platform. Displayed in an open lunch-bucket – no lunch inside. Weaving beautiful patterns for my ladie to wear on her fingers. Admirers aplenty – not one has an extra dime.

Fingers fly on the keys - sitting there on a shelf - couldn't believe the sight - not one in a thousand - little boy grew up - somewhere in the mountains - shaking out the cobwebs - witnessed three storms - observing and recording - the world's second-largest.

Music and carpentry work. Used to work at night on the house. It was all they could afford, but he fixed it up.
He used to play the concertina. Make his fingers fly on the keys. He could play any tune if someone would whistle it first.
Now the concertina sits there on a shelf on the library table. It's called that because it has shelves for books. Nobody in the family knows how to play.

There was no earthquake or tornado that day.
No one's elbow gave it a nudge while tending the fire.

Sleeping on a boxcar in the mountains. Black sky with not a star. Hundreds of hoboes on the train. Couldn't believe the sight as we slowly pulled out of the yards. Watched the others to see how it's done. You lie down on the running board, see? That board that runs the length of the roof of the car? You hook your pack so it's safe on your arm, like this, then you sit on the running board, pull your blanket up over your head, hook your elbows down at your sides – see? – and pull your feet in close to the board and you lie back down. You can sleep like this for hours. Snug and safe and warm. Don't worry! Not one in a thousand ever rolls off! You'll wake up to the frost all 'round you in a line!

A man playing a fiddle while everyone sings.
Sourdough sizzling on a small iron stove.

John Passfield

Green grass, flowing rivers, shining apples.

Friday July 15 1932 - Saturday July 16 1932 - Sunday July 17 1932 - Monday July 18 1932 - Tuesday July 19 1932 - Wednesday July 20 1932 - Thursday July 21 1932.

Ski in the mountains every winter?
Salmon jumping in the streams?
Further away than London, England from Ontario?

"The little boy grew up and gathered flowers for his mom and watched for his dad to come home at the end of every day."

Oak Lake - Virdon - Kirkella - Moosimin - Whitewood - Broadview - Grenfell - Wolsley - Indian Head - Qu'appelle - Regina - Pence - Asqua - Moose Jaw - Caron - Chaplin - Rush Lake - Swift Current - Java - Seward.

A sing-song around an old piano.
A bottle of whiskey and a ten dollar bill.
Water trickling down the face of a rock.

Perched on top of a boxcar. Somewhere in the mountains. Moving slowly up a steep grade. Can't believe what I'm seeing! A man rolling off a boxcar! About twenty-five boxcars ahead! Rolling right off the roof of the boxcar and onto the ground! He's lying there on the stone at the side of the rails. Slowly our boxcar moves towards where he tumbled off. He rolls over onto his knees. Must be shaking out the cobwebs. Must have been sound asleep and the train gave a lurch and he tumbled off. Now he's standing up and waving up at the train. Some of the hoboes wave right back and I do too. Other are sleeping and don't know what's going on. The ground must be soft and he must have been loose. And we're only going slow. Must be people roll off the trains and don't stand up and laugh and wave. Someone tosses off his pack and he walks along and bends to pick it up.

Stayed in Revelstoke one day. Saw the worlds 2nd largest engine, the 8000 type, of the C.P.R. Made a couple of stews and took pictures. Left on a drag that night. Witnessed three storms roll up the valley, and disperse before reaching us.

"Of course, each of these stations is limited to recording the weather which is true of its own situation and at the time of the collection of the data."

"Young architects, accountants, engineers and physicians are out of work."

Meat, potatoes, vegetables, fruit. Pass your plate and dad will cut a slice of beef. Plenty of vegetables from the garden. The weather has been so good this year. Today, the mother baked a special cake.

Nettles in my hand - the importance of the sun - wait for the boil - haunted by nightmares - quiet dreams - head sunk on a pillow - what the country's like - the shooting pain - dark as can be - just a light-bulb.

You know a lot of people don't know how to write or read. They would get letters from the old country from a brother or someone like that. And my dad would read the words that the brother wrote.

And then they didn't know how to write back. Never learned to write at all. Too busy earning a living to go to school.

So we would go to people's houses on a Sunday. My dad would take me along. And he would listen to what they say and write it down.

Your father lies somewhere
under the earth
in a grave.

Staying in Revelstoke for a day. Seeing the world's second-largest steam engine. The eight-thousand type of the CPR. Making ourselves a couple of stews. Taking pictures of Charlie and me. Catching a slow freight and leaving the yards in the middle of the night. Watching the sun coming up at dawn. Seeing storms rolling up through the valleys. Lots of sheep on all the hillsides, though the grass looks dry.

Rode all day on the train; country very arid, but some good scenery. Lots of sheep range in the Selkirk range. Placed my hand on a cactus, had nettles in my hand for two weeks afterward. Country resembles Mexico as I picture it. sand and stones and beautiful flowers.

"As the sun gave heat and light, it was thought, for many generations, that it was the centre of the universe."

The two boys are exhausted, so they stop and take a break. Time to relax and boil their pot and have some stew. Water trickling out of a stream. Carrots and potatoes and few bits of meat. They gather some brush and start the fire and wait for the boil. They gather more brush and blow on the flame, but the pot doesn't boil. No matter how much they build up the flames the water won't boil. A mushy, luke-warm stew and then more hours of slipping and sliding on the face of the rock.

Picking nettles from my palm.
Dodging stray bullets.

Bullets whizzing by - things are awful quiet - a thick Cumberland brogue - going home flat broke - lurching to a stop - up on his shoulders - all that I can remember - very musical man - came home every night - live without the donkey.

And I would sit there on a chair while my dad did the writing. The people would give me a little biscuit and a cup of tea.

And I would listen to my dad's voice as he talked with all these people. All the people from the old country who couldn't read and write. And I would listen to them talk as I sipped my tea.

And sometimes he would bring the concertina. Or they'd have an old fiddle in the house and my dad would play. All those old songs from the old country that the people had sung back home for hundreds of years.

Not haunted by nightmares.
All he knows are quiet dreams.
Head sunk on a pillow or cradled in hay.

Riding all day on the train. Lots of sheep in the Selkirk range. Very arid, very dry. Don't think of desert terrain in BC, but here it is. Sand and stone and beautiful flowers. Like the Mexico I've heard about all these years. Going down through a cut. Stopping to check for a hotbox. Charlie and me climbing up to get a look at what the country's like out here. Putting my hand down smack on a cactus! Can't believe the shooting pain! Thousands of nettles in my hand! Charlie helping me back on the train. Charlie helping pick the nettles out of my hand.

2:50 - 2:51 - 2:52 - 2:53 - 2:54 - 2:55 - 2:56 - 2:57 - 2:58 - 2:59 - 3:00 - 3:01 - 3:02 - 3:03 - 3:04 - 3:05 - 3:06 - 3:07 - 3:08 - 3:09 - 3:10 - 3:11 - 3:12 - 3:13 - 3:14 - 3:15 - 3:16 - 3:17 - 3:18 - 3:19 - 3:20 - 3:21 - 3:22 - 3:23 - 3:24 - 3:25 - 3:26 - 3:27 - 3:28 - 3:29 - 3:30 - 3:31.

An old man
rumbling
in a thick Cumberland brogue.

A ploughman driving an eight-horse plough.
The immense size of the known universe.
A train speeding past water rocks and trees.

A younger man
writing a letter
as the old man talks.

Get yourself a seaman's card?
Sail wherever the oceans go?
Enjoy the best of every city in the world?

A young boy
sitting
with a biscuit and a cup of tea.

    The train is stopping for water. Somewhere near Red Deer, as far as we can tell. Dark as can be outside. Just a light-bulb on a pole at the end of the yards. Wonder where we can get some food? Let's swing down here and have a look 'round. Swinging down out of the boxcar and swinging right back up again! What the heck was that noise? Do you know what that sounded like! A big loud 'ping' on the side of the boxcar! Sounds like bullets whizzing by! We peak around the corner and there's a big old Ford bucking frantically across the tracks! Just leaping over the tracks – coming straight at us! We duck back into the corner and lie down flat on the floor! A few more shots and a few more pings on the side of the car! The headlights glare inside our boxcar! The car goes roaring by! We lie still and things are awful quiet for a while. Then a lurch and the train starts moving. We stay down in the corner and listen as the train moves through the yards. Moving slowly and picking up speed. The both of us keeping well away from the door.

Chapter 6

Having a drink at the Great Divide. Swinging down off the train and reading the sign. Canadian Pacific Railway. Altitude 5,332 feet. One foot in Alberta and one foot in British Columbia. Pour a pail of water on one side and it runs to the Atlantic Ocean. Pour a pail of water on the other side and it runs to the Pacific Ocean. Slopes of pine trees, snow in the valleys, jagged peaks. Sunshine, cool breeze, a wheezing train. Sitting on a rock and chomping on a sandwich and smelling the freshness of the air. Looking North, South, East and West. Another bite of the sandwich and another swig of the drink. Every mountain top is below us. Every valley heads down to the sea. Top of the world until the engineer pulls the whistle. Swinging back up onto the train and we're off again.

A drink at the Great Divide.

An apple stinging a hobo in the neck.
A brake-stick snapping as railcars crash together.
Two boys struggling to climb a slope of shale.

Climbed Sulphur Mt.

A tired mother reading a novel in an easy-chair.
A large crowd at a dance on Saturday night.
Sunlight on the needles of a forest.

Riot of colour uptown.

Suppose you were a twin?
Two people who both were you?
What would that other person be?

3:32 - 3:33 - 3:34 - 3:35 - 3:36 - 3:37 - 3:38 - 3:39 - 3:40 - 3:41- 3:42 - 3:43 - 3:44 - 3:45 - 3:46 - 3:47 - 3:48 - 3:49 - 3:50 - 3:51 - 3:52 - 3:53 - 3:54

- 3:55 - 3:56 - 3:57 - 3:58 - 3:59 - 4:00 - 4:01 - 4:02 - 4:03 - 4:04 - 4:05 - 4:06 - 4:07 - 4:08 - 4:09 - 4:10 - 4:11 - 4:12 - 4:13.

A tall story at Field. Not knowing whether to believe it or not. Stopping for four hours in the afternoon. Buying provisions and talking to a man who works in the round-house. See, they work on the trains in here and then when they're ready to drive 'em outside they got no fire in the boiler to make the steam. So they pump air into the boiler. Acts like steam and drives the pistons and moves the wheels. Well, sir, they put one out on the siding one time and forgot to let out the air. So they're working here in the shop and the telegraph starts rattlin' and there's an operator at the other end of the line, in a village about sixteen miles from here, and he's sayin' he's just seen a ghost! A locomotive ghost! No smoke comin' out of the smokestack and no engineer inside and she passed right in front of his eyes and went right on by!

Stopped four hours in the afternoon at Field. bought provisions to continue the trip. Washed up in the Columbia river. Cop sent the boys uptown to eat. (Bum their meals.) Stopped and had a drink at the Great Divide. B.C. and Alta. Left freight on the fly, to get to Banff.

"It us now accepted as fact that the earth was formed when a ball of gas was condensed to form the solid globe with which we are now familiar."

Wandering in a desert! Some kind of covering on my face! Just my eyes free to see and they're not much good! The wind keeps blowing stronger! Sand blowing hard against my robes! Thirsty as thirsty can be! Could be miles from any water! All I can feel is this grit between my teeth! Shoulda stayed at the oasis! No hint of a path, but trying to walk as straight as I can! What if I'm going sideways? What if I'm going in circles? When will this wind die down? I can barely see my feet when I try to look down!

"The collapse of the Kreditanstalt Bank in Austria is having wide-reaching effects in the rest of the world."

Reading the sign - pour a pail of water - the freshness of the air - top of the world - riot of colour - whether to believe - right in front of your eyes - not all the gases solidified - as thirsty as can be - I'm going sideways.

Went to elementary school. Elmdale School until grade eight. Then on to the high school uptown.
About a year of that and I'd had enough. Anxious to get out and work. If any good job came along, I'd be sure to take it.
Always had a paper route. Since I was about ten. Worked my way up to better jobs as time went on.

*Chances are
your future
will be cloud.*

Standing beside the tracks and looking down. The fireman thought we'd like to see it. Asked the engineer to stop. Looking down into the canyon. Nine hundred feet straight down. A locomotive wedged in the rocks. The bulk of it still intact. Surrounded by scattered debris. Just like those dinosaurs they find way back in the hills. Went off the rails years ago and been there ever since. No way to get it back up here. Gonna be there for a pretty long time. A lot can happen when you're workin' on the trains. Just one question we don't ask and neither the engineer or the fireman mentions the topic. Was there someone inside when the train went off the rails?

Climbed Sulpher Mt. in Banff, took six hours. 2 ½ hrs to go up the face. Alti 7490'. Cold clammy wind blew on the summit, mosquitoes in clouds. observatory on top, and book to register. top of Mt. was loose shale and rocks. Had dinner (a stew) in the descent, moss heavy near the summit.

"A good map will always contain a note indicating which element – area or shape – the cartographer has chosen to distort."

Watching the waters part.
Listening to a story.

Trudging through a desert! Miles and miles of nothing but sand! Up ahead I see a speck, but what can it be? Sticking up out of the sand! Is it palm trees and vegetation? Trudging as fast as I can manage! My sandals sinking down lower with every step! It is! It is an oasis! I remember the taste of water now! The grit between my teeth will be washed away! So cool and wet in the bowl of my throat! I'll wade and splash and swim! I'll drink 'til my stomach's bursting! Trying to run in the sand! All I want is a drink and to rest for a spell in the shade!

Going in circles - worked my way up - surrounded by scattered debris - a lot can happen - one question we don't ask - if a map has a true shape - if its areas are correct - it is an oasis - all i want is a drink - something to do.

I'd go with my mom to these big houses. Walk the length of the town. Carry the food into the kitchen and then go home.
Couldn't help her clean the houses. Just my mother was wanted inside. I'd go out and try to find some work to do.
Always seemed to find something to do. Worked at the ice-house from

fall to spring. Then Charlie and me would work all summer on the Anderson farm.

> *"I have come in search of truth," said the woodsman.*
> *He glanced around at all the other trees.*
> *"I was told that this is where to look for truth."*

Climbing up Sulphur Mountain. Having a heck of a time. Our feet keep slipping and sliding on the loose shale. Exhausted, so we stop to boil our kettle and have some stew. Water from the stream and carrots and potatoes and meat. No matter how much we build up the flames, the water just won't boil. Cold stew and a few more hours of slipping and sliding.

> *A desert in the middle of the mountains.*
> *Old letters left behind in an abandoned cabin.*
> *A box filled with wood-working tools.*

> *Friday July 22 1932 - Saturday July 23 1932 - Sunday July 24 1932 - Monday July 25 1932 - Tuesday July 26 1932 - Wednesday July 27 1932.*

What is the self you carry with you?
What are the selves you leave behind?
Are there different selves for the soil on which you grow?

"And then one day the boy's father died and now there was just the mom and her five children."

> *Gull Lake - Crowe Lake - Maple Creek - Walsh - Dunmore - Medicine Hat - Redcliff - Bowell - Suffield - Alderson - Kininvie - Bantry - Cassils - Bassano - Langdon - Shepherd - Ogden - Calgary - Cochrane - Morley.*

> *A group of applicants in a waiting room.*
> *Mounties slapping their truncheons in their hands.*
> *A pot of stew boiling in the railroad yards.*

Swimming in the hot springs at Banff. Hot and cold water pools. Going back and forth from one to the other. Can't believe the size of the pool. Do a lot of swimming at home but couldn't swim the length of this pool. The hot water saps your energy. All you want to do is relax. Just relax and let the tension flow out of your bones. Plenty of tourists in this park. Ask about jobs, but there don't seem to be any. All the jobs have been taken up. So we relax for the day and act like tourists ourselves.

> *Had a swim in the cave and basin, walked to the park, saw elk, Buffalo*

etc. Tried to hop a freight; going too fast; hit the highway, for ten miles in the Mountains, was picked up by a bus driver and rode 75 miles to the Palliser Hotel.

"Generally, data is collected by the local station four times a day, as weather is constantly changing."

"The Canadian government debt accounts for two-thirds of the country's current revenue."

At last a pool of water! I kick my sandals off and wade in the shallows! Ahhh, the coolness on my toes! Such a soothing balm on my ankles! I bend over and cup my hands! So cool in the shade of these trees! And I was thinking of giving up! Walking for miles and not a drop of water to find! Suddenly here it is! I raise my hands to my lips! The water dribbles through my fingers! I purse my lips to drink, but the wind picks up! What a strange sensation! All the water blows away! I can't understand what's happening! I can't seem to quench my thirst! I scoop my hands again, but I can't seem to manage to drink! The wind is so strong that it blows all the water away!

In search of truth - a heck of a time - the size of the pool - act like tourists - observations are taken - a soothing balm - thinking of giving up - the water blows away - can't seem to manage - looked in the garden.

Delivered groceries all over town. First for Witherspoon and then for Durnan and Spry. Always made sure the ponies and horses were nicely groomed.
Charlie and me both worked with horses. Helped out old Doc Palmer. Worked with Ben Powers on his farm.
Toronto Exhibition, New York State, Montreal. But that was all volunteer – no money there. We'd ride in the horse-cars and we always bought our own meals.

Jimmy looked in the garden for his little red ball.
His mother and his siblings helped him look.

The Calgary Stampede. Chuck wagon races and flap jacks and ridin' and ropin' the bulls. Hundreds of people in the stands and the microphone crackling. Couple of jobs I wouldn't want, but it's fun to watch. Cowboys riding down the streets and lassoing girls. Masked varmints riding into the banks and sticking them up. Everybody wearing Stetsons. Guess we must look like we're from the East. Man with a bullwhip shredding a potato sack. Then he brings out this tiny girl. Putting a cigarette in her mouth as we walk away.

Stampede. Riot of colour uptown, Cowboys singing, roping and riding. Parade of Indians. Chuck-wagons, cooking flapjacks on the main drag. Big Stampede parade, everything pertaining to the West. Wild horses, red river carts, Prairie schooners, floats etc.

"When humankind was able to see beyond the sun, it was revealed that the sun was part of a larger entity."

She sits on the verandah on a Sunday afternoon. She listens as her youngest daughter reads. "Hi Mom. Still on the bum. We're going to move on to Len Yarwood's in Alberta and see if he has work for us. We're seeing all kinds of things and meeting all kinds of people. The prairies and the mountains are everything I figured they would be. Sorry to have to write home from Vancouver and ask for Ken to send out some of my money. That wasn't the original plan. Sorry about the fence. I know I said I'd fix it, but me and Charlie left in a hurry so there wasn't time. Tell Ken to do what he can for now and I'll build a whole new fence when I get home. I'll send you an address just as soon as we have one. We'll buckle down out here and make ourselves some money before we come home."

Climbing the face of a mountain.
Buying a white Stetson.

This is not the case - all kinds of things - the original plan - there wasn't time - there was a fortune teller - never said a word - take turns going inside - lay the ticket down - dazzles my eyes - the edge of a garden.

We were down at Port Stanley one time. Down at the beach after a swim. We'd cool off after bringing in hay on the Anderson farm.
And there was a fortune teller there. Madame Florina, I think it was. And Charlie said why don't we go have our fortunes read?
I don't know what she said to Charlie. He's never said a word. But she told me that I would never have to worry about money: "You'll never be rich but you shall never be in want."

He put his arms inside the arms,
He put his legs inside the legs,
He put his head inside the head of the puppeteer.

Getting my fortune at the Stampede. A Hindu shoving spikes through his nose and through a hole in his tongue. Not interesting to me, but I give the girl my dime. Have to wait through his act with the spike before he settles down to business. Then we line up at the tent and take turns going inside. No spikes are on the table. Not even a crystal ball. Just the Hindu, a bare wooden table and a pack of cards. He never touches the cards. Just waves me to sit in the seat and studies my eyes. Am I supposed to ask him a question? About what my future's going to be? I lay the ticket down. The Hindu stares and stares and stares. Before I can say what I'm here for, he clears his throat. Doesn't sound all that much like a Hindu. More of a croak than a human voice. You'll never be rich but you'll always have enough. He takes the ticket and drops it into a pail beside his seat. He stands up, so I stand up and leave the tent. The sun is so bright it almost dazzles my eyes.

3:32 - 3:33 - 3:34 - 3:35 - 3:36 - 3:37 - 3:38 - 3:39 - 3:40 - 3:41 - 3:42 - 3:43 - 3:44 - 3:45 - 3:46 - 3:47 - 3:48 - 3:49 - 3:50 - 3:51 - 3:52 - 3:53 - 3:54 - 3:55 - 3:56 - 3:57 - 3:58 - 3:59 - 4:00 - 4:01 - 4:02 - 4:03 - 4:04 - 4:05 - 4:06 - 4:07 - 4:08 - 4:09 - 4:10 - 4:11 - 4:12 - 4:13.

*A fence
running around
the edge of a garden.*

*A concertina sitting on a shelf.
A dog with a mouth like an alligator.
A miller grinding grain into flour.*

*A gate
with a pair of hinges
and a latch.*

What does the seed bring to the soil?
What does the soil bring to the seed?
Would an oak grow straight or crooked in different soil?

*A hole
in the fence
about the size of a rabbit.*

Standing in front of a mirror. Wishing I was a little more tanned. More tanned than we were, but not quite Western yet. Store full of cowboy gear. Some of it more for tourists. Putting the hat on my head and taking it off and putting it on again. A big white Stetson just like everybody wears in the movies. Hoot Gibson, Broncho Billy, Tom Mix. Glancing around the store. Charlie looking at a pair of boots in the front window. Don't' mind Charlie looking at me, but don't want the clerk to think I'm vain. Turning around and checking the look. A couple of wind-burned cowpokes coming in. Spurs jingling as they walk. Both of them wearing black Stetsons. Maybe white will get too dirty when I'm working on the ranches. Still I have to buy me a white one. That's what all the cowboys wear in the movies. Can't see myself wearing black. Black is for bad guys; white is for good. Just hope no one laughs when they see me out ridin' the range.

Chapter 7

A dance at the Palliser Hotel. Me and Charlie getting spruced up and going downtown. Can't believe how big an affair. All the streets roped off for blocks. Wax on the streets to make them slippery. Shaking soap powder out of a box so we can dance. Fifteen hundred people dancing. Pouring in and out of the lobby. Non-stop music with rotating bands. Over a million dollars to build it. Eleven stories high. The most luxurious of all the hotels in the West. A bet with Charlie as to who can dance the most times.

Gathered our belongings.

A cowboy with his leg in a plaster cast.
A boy who lives in a perfect town.
Swimmers lying down on a grassy slope.

Five shots passed us.

Lining-up for tobacco at the work-camp canteen.
Striking workers huddling around a burning barrel.
Help-wanted ads with stubby-pencil marks.

All the big fairs in the West.

What is there, do you think, about horses that interests you?
Are you their servant or their master?
Their rider or their groom?

4:14 - 4:15 - 4:16 - 4:17 - 4:18 - 4:19 - 4:20 - 4:21 - 4:22 - 4:23 - 4:24 - 4:25 - 4:26 - 4:27 - 4:28 - 4:29 - 4:30 - 4:31- 4:32 - 4:33 - 4:34 - 4:35 - 4:36 - 4:37 - 4:38 - 4:39 - 4:40 - 4:41- 4:42 - 4:43 - 4:44 - 4:45 - 4:46 - 4:47 - 4:48 - 4:49 - 4:50 - 4:51- 4:52 - 4:53 - 4:54 - 4:55.

An offer of a job! With the Johnny J. Jones Expeditions! You know that girl with the rodeo show? Heading off to the Edmonton Fair? She tells me her father might take us on. Might be some work for you two! You say you know horses! I'll ask my father if he can find something for you and your friend! There's ten or fifteen cowboys. They ride and rope and put on a show. We wouldn't be performers, she says. We'd be tending the horses and mules. Putting up the tents and cooking the stew. They're hitting every town all over the West. Travel all night in those beat-up old trucks and set up in the day. She seems all right, but hard to tell about her father. Didn't look too happy with the take when he passed the hat. Hate to work for a couple of weeks and then not get paid.

Today we gathered our belongings. To hit the trail once more. Also done our washing, including overalls and caps. Attended the street dance at the Palliser Hotel. 1,500 people dancing.

"Since the earth cooled, the materials of which it is composed have undergone numerous changes which are detectable by scientific means."

Two Studebakers in the shed where the hens all lay their eggs. Siphoning the last of the gasoline from the one that works. Brought the first one home brand-new and got racin' around in the barnyard. Hit the fence-post and broke a wheel and towed her into the chicken shed and bought another one in town and drove her home. Now there's two of them here in the shed with the chickens nestin' in the seats and leavin' their eggs.

"The minor economic rally of 1931 now seems to be at an end."

Offer of a job - tending the horses and mules - hitting every town - not get paid - work for a couple of weeks - undergone considerable changes - last of the gasoline - attended the street dance - nestin' in the seats - brought our money home.

Grew a moustache when I was nineteen, so I would look older. Went over to the railroad to apply for a job. If you're Robert's boy, of course we have a job!

Everybody in the family was working. Brought our money home to our mom. I even bought a car – a '27 Chev.

Then this Depression came along. Every factory was laying off. The railroad cut us down to a couple of days a month.

The rain will ease down in soaking sheets.
More than I can believe.

Difficult time getting out of Calgary. Spending the afternoon in the yards. Finding the track we want to follow, but no trains for a while. About twenty hoboes waiting. Talking with some of them for a while. Chased off the stock-trains by the bulls. Twenty railroad bulls came in cars and told us the train wasn't gonna pull out 'til we all climbed down! A chance at a ride we don't really want. A circus train going slowly, easy to jump on, but a gang of mean-looking ruffians drinking, at a card game, inside a cage. With what we know about roustabouts, we let it pass.

Left in afternoon for the yards; got located. 20 Bo's waiting, were chased off stock train by bulls, about twenty of them, in cars. Drifted back again to sleep and wait for another. The circus train looked too formidable, so let it pass.

"One should try to imagine the earth as a hollow glass sphere with lines of longitude and latitude drawn around its circumference."

Dancing in the street.
Keeping out of jail.

The sun throws a young man's shadow on the frosted glass. "Come in," calls Madame Florina. "You are here to have your fortune read, of course." "Just wondering about the future," the young man says. "My friend tells me that you can say what will come to pass."

Railroad cut us down - rain will ease down - inside a cage - principal of map projection - visualize the globe - young man's shadow - wondering about the future - what will come to pass - everything slowed right down - could be your last.

Worked in gravel pits and construction. I was a mover for quite a while. Moving everything from furniture to cows.
But everything slowed right down. Everybody was laying off. Every day you worked on a job could be your last.
Oh I've done all kinds of jobs, but they all keep petering out. This is the Depression, you know, and everybody's laying off. Couple of days or a couple of weeks is all you get.

Dig the foundation deep.
Check the batter-boards for square.

Arriving in Edmonton Sunday night. Charlie and me with our overalls on. Figuring it's wise to look like trainmen when we get to the yards. About twenty or thirty men. All of them came in on our train and all are going somewhere different. Standing around and trading lore. Where are you going and where have you been? Where did you eat and where did you sleep? How are the railroad police in each city? Which track do we want in these yard to go West, North or South? Suddenly there's a commotion. A bunch of cops arrive on the scene. Hard to tell if they're mean or not. We sidle over to the edge of the bunch. Charlie and me in our railroad duds. The cops round them all up and march them away. Wonder what they'll do with them all? Put them in jail or give them a meal? Every place we come to is different. Maybe we made a mistake in wearing our overalls.

A dead horse being dragged to a bone pile.
A man with a beard like Father Christmas.
A lady snipping roses for a vase.

Thursday July 28 1932 - Friday July 29 1932 - Saturday July 30 1932 - Sunday July 31 1932 - Monday August 1 1932 - Tuesday August 2 1932 - Wednesday August 3 1932.

What are the jumps that you take them over?
What are the pits into which you could fall?
Who is actually taking the jump – the horse or you?

"The mother catered to people's parties and cleaned people's houses and the kids all went to school."

Banff - Lake Louise - Field - Golden - Donald - Beavermouth - Connaught Tunnel - Kicking Horse Pass - Revelstoke - Taft - Craigellachie - Sicamous - Salmon Arm - Shuswai - Pritchard - Kamloops - Tranquille - Savour - Ashcroft - Spencer Bridge.

Church workers packing food, clothing and fruit.
A little boy chasing a bubble across the grass.
An old lady knitting a baby-blanket.

Sitting in the back of a car surrounded by flowers. The whole car loaded with flowers. Helping to take them to the fair. Four days in Edmonton at a house that is more like a mansion. Mrs. Marshall and her husband. Chief of police for the whole of Alberta. She says she's writing a book. All about hoboes and hobo slang and how we beg and do work for food and ride the rails. We each of us have a marble sink – I have green and Charlie has black. A couple of swanky rooms above the garage. Trying to tell her we're not really hoboes. Just a couple of railroad workers out of work. Just touring the West and trying to earn some cash. Says she'll put us in the book, though, just the same. She gives us a whole roll of tickets to spend at the fair. It's a heck of a lotta fun but we're not making any money. She slows down and turns in at the gate and the car bumps up on the curb and the flowers all sway all around us on the seat.

Caught passenger train at the bridge, rode to Red Deer. Some one on the tender fired five shots passed us. No casualtys. A high powered car chased two fellows into the bush. Cop at Red Deer referred us to the R. House for a wash up. Arrived at Edmonton Sun. Night. Cops took 30 men, missed us.

"When the four observations are placed together, one can see the development of local weather trends."

"The burden of this depression is falling on the families, the unskilled and the young."

A group of people gathered in a tiny parlour. Envelopes and letters on the table. All is quiet as a man begins to read. Cheerful chatter as they talk about the news. Pen and inkwell and sheets of paper. Envelopes and a couple of stamps. A man talking slowly in a Cumberland brogue. He pauses and watches the pen move on the page.

Going somewhere different - sidle over to the edge - maybe we made a mistake - surrounded by flowers - not really hoboes - put us in the book - a whole roll of tickets - fired five shots - known as 'synoptic' hours - pen move on the page.

Went to Michigan to stay with my sister, Margaret, and my brother, Bob. They both had steady work 'cause they'd been there for years. Before this Depression, there used to be plenty of jobs.

A paint-checker for Essex cars. Checking for flaws in the panels. If you find a flaw, it's painted all over again.

Blowing up stumps for a highway near Mt. Clemens. You touch a wire to the steering wheel of an old Ford. Blow the stumps clean out of the way where the highway will go.

Working the counter at a restaurant. Shout into a tube and the food appears from below. Employee discount for a piece of key lime pie.

Escorting the lady who took the cash down the street to the bank. Attacked one day on the sidewalk as we were walking along. Held them off 'til the cops came and the restaurant owner bought me a brand-new hat.

Wisdom is invisible;
it has no seed nor soil.

Vermillion. The train station. Thought we'd never arrive alive. Local freight going thirty-five miles an hour. Spent a torturous day on top. Broiling sun and we made every stop. Questioned by a Mountie at Vegreville. Arrived in Vermillion at six p.m. Asking the Station Agent how to get to Len Yarwood's place. Fourteen miles straight across the prairie. No transportation whatsoever. Fourteen miles across the prairie and we'll have to walk. Starting off down the tracks. The afternoon closing down. Getting dark.

Had shower at Y. M. C. A. called up Mrs. Marshall; met her at the "Bay". Drove around town. Saw Capitol buildings. Golf courses etc. Had diner, met Mr. Marshall. Accompanied Mrs. Marshal to the fair, stayed till late at night. Johnny J. Jones Exposition Shows. Play at all the big fairs in the West.

"Observation of the heavens indicated that the sun is only one of many stars, perhaps numbering in the billions."

A heavy mist this morning. Too wet to work today. He sits on a bench on the porch with some leather, some twine and an awl and works away. He is making a couple of bridles. Figures he'll need a flexible size. A gentle neighing comes from the barnyard. The colts are stretching their legs. They cavort like a couple of puppies. Too young to break to lead. Too headstrong to pull the cart. He punches at the leather with the awl.

> Riding in a car full of flowers.
> Sleeping beside a warm stove.

Checking for flaws - painted all over again - clean out of the way - food appears from below - never arrive alive - no transportation whatsoever - small star among millions - guide them with your knees - pure poetry - numbers on the blackboard.

Joined the militia at Battle Creek. Liked the military life and grooming the horses. Just a month of training in case of another war.
So here's where the horses come in again. Walk, trot, canter – whatever you ask them to do. You don't ever yank at their mouth – you have to learn to guide them with your knees.
Taking them up and over the jumps. Charlie and me assisting Ben Powers at the Royal Winter Fair. Pure poetry when you're riding a beautiful horse.

> *The reaper reaps the grain in the field.*
> *What he is and what he does is his gift.*

Striking out across the prairie. Finding the trail that takes the direction we're supposed to go. We come up to the top of a hill and it takes our breath away. Two Alberta deer! Two big, grey Alberta deer! Ten or fifteen feet away! Standing in the middle of the trail and nuzzling each other! We stand silently and watch. They don't see us. Don't know we're here. A beautiful sight! Truly beautiful! Finally, they sense our presence and sprint away.

4:14 - 4:15 - 4:16 - 4:17 - 4:18 - 4:19 - 4:20 - 4:21 - 4:22 - 4:23 - 4:24 - 4:25 - 4:26 - 4:27 - 4:28 - 4:29 - 4:30 - 4:31- 4:32 - 4:33 - 4:34 - 4:35 - 4:36 - 4:37 - 4:38 - 4:39 - 4:40 - 4:41- 4:42 - 4:43 - 4:44 - 4:45 - 4:46 - 4:47 - 4:48 - 4:49 - 4:50 - 4:51- 4:52 - 4:53 - 4:54 - 4:55.

A man
lying
on a couch on a porch.

A section man fixing railroad tracks.
Angels hovering and flapping their wings.
The people who inhabit the globe.

His breathing
slow and steady
as a watch.

What is the poetry in the jumping at the fair?
What is the poetry in pulling the cart filled with coal?
Have you ever worked with a horse that you actually owned?

Occasionally
a gargle
in his throat.

Walking across the prairie. In the direction we're supposed to take. Late in the day and hard to see. It's July, but it's cold and dark. Coming across a schoolhouse. The door is on the latch and it's warm inside. Must have had a meeting in here 'cause the fire is still in the stove! A break if ever there was one! Maybe they'll come back soon, but no one arrives. Big pot-bellied stove with a long, warm stovepipe. Some numbers on the blackboard. Greek to us. Getting pretty cold outside. Unrolling our blankets on the floor near the fire. Settling down for a nice warm sleep. Tomorrow, we'll get up early and look for Len.

Chapter 8

Up at six o'clock. The pot-bellied stove is still warm. Hate to leave this warm schoolhouse, though we have nothing to eat or drink. Striking out in the general direction where we were told we should find Len. Passing through dense bushes. 'Chaparral' they call it. Passing bands of cattle. Wonder if they all belong to Len? Well he's got a lot of acreage. Len and his brother too. A mixture of animals and crops, so they could be his. We must be somewhere near his homestead. We've been walking since six o'clock. There's a lotta miles between farms out here in the West.

Maps and diverse directions.

A line-rider trailing seven horses.
A traveller waving down a car on the road.
An old fellow telling many stories.

Eye us in alarm.

A bear catching salmon in a stream.
Prairie wheat waving in the wind.
A train moving slowly through a mountain pass.

Striking a dim trail.

Why is the Great Divide so narrow?
Why so easy to step across?
Why did you linger there for only a moment's time?

4:56 - 4:57 - 4:58 - 4:59 - 5:00 - 5:01 - 5:02 - 5:03 - 5:04 - 5:05 - 5:06 - 5:07 - 5:08 - 5:09 - 5:10 - 5:11 - 5:12 - 5:13 - 5:14 - 5:15 - 5:16 - 5:17 - 5:18 - 5:19 - 5:20 - 5:21 - 5:22 - 5:23 - 5:24 - 5:25 - 5:26 - 5:27 - 5:28 - 5:29 - 5:30 - 5:31- 5:32 - 5:33 - 5:34 - 5:35 - 5:36 - 5:37 - 5:38.

Encountering bands of cattle. They seem uneasy to see a human. Rising up to their feet and eyeing us in alarm. Arming ourselves with stout clubs. No trees to climb and these clubs won't stop a stampede. Moving stealthily past the herds along the trail. The trail is faint and dim, but it's all we have to go by. Probably not too often that Len goes into town. Skirting around the edge of a slough. Bursting out into a clearing. A house and a fence and a barn. Walking out into the open and the man fixing the fence turns out to be Len!

Had a shower and breakfast. Started to enquire way out of town. Got maps and diverse directions. Met an old Hoboe, and were put on the right track. Slept in signal tower all night. Undisturbed by trains crossing the diamond in the night.

"The layer below the earth's crust seems to be composed of a material which is somewhere between a solid and a liquid, as it flows like a slowly-moving river."

He puts a check-mark beside each number, but things still don't add up right. Sixty cents a bushel. Twelve bushel to the acre. Mortgage, seed, machinery. What's owed to the bank. If you get a good crop, the price of wheat goes down.

"Canadian exports are down over sixty-two percent of what they were before the economic crisis."

In the general direction - we must be somewhere - diverse directions - a dim trail - eyeing us in alarm - skirting about the edge - on the right track - a zone of material - it appears to flow - don't add up right.

Jobs back home around St. Thomas. Lots of workers and not many jobs. For every call to work there was dozens of guys lined up.

A bit of work on the Anderson farm, a bit of work for Lover's Movers, a bit of work hauling gravel to construction sites.

Tried making cupboards for people, but I never made a dime. I'd buy the wood and not get my money back. Nowadays, nobody has money to pay.

Drove a millionaire to Toronto one afternoon. His chauffer was down with the flu. The limousine heater caught fire and we almost perished in flames.

The load is much heavier
now the donkey's dead.

Helping Len with his chores. Buckets of water, bags of grain. Up in the morning collecting eggs. Got a whole section of land. My brother's got one too. Six hundred acres each. That's a pretty good spread. Adjoining homesteads. His idea to come out West. If it was me, I'd still be back on the Anderson farm. Good to see you guys again. Good memories of St. Thomas, but I'm better off here. This fence we're putting in will be mine alone. No more working for someone else like I did in England.

Caught local going about 35 per. Ten missed it, one man turned complete somersault. Spent tortuous day on top, in broiling sun, made every stop. Vegreville – questioned by Mountie, arrived Vermillion at 6 p. m. Walked track 7 miles, cut across country 3 miles, lost direction slightly; So stayed at school house all night.

"If one imagines a light inside the glass sphere, the lines of longitude and latitude can be imagined as projected onto a piece of flat paper."

Avoiding hostile cattle.
Finding a home-town friend.

What's wrong with me, I wonder? Same willow, same size branch. Same knife as I always use. Same pattern I always whittle to make a flute.

A bit of work - never made a dime - almost perished in flames - good memories - be mine alone - working for someone else - spent tortuous day - allowed to shine - same pattern - so we all get along.

So Margaret and Bob are over in Detroit and Mt. Clemens. Hilda is at the Alma College and Ken at the shoe factory. Both in town.

So we all get along pretty good. Everybody gives money to Mom. Doesn't spend it on herself – just puts it in the bank.

Mom is making out all right. Says she doesn't need any help. Says the catering and the cleaning is fine with her.

When it fell it broke into pieces.
The fragments were scattered all over the floor.

Over to dinner with the Cartwrights. Len's girlfriend's parents' place. Ten of us around the table for a prairie feast. Oh, we been out here many years. Came out here when we was just kids. Just got married and headed off to homestead way out West. Our daughter was born out here. It's all she's ever known. Nice that she and Len get along so well. The farms are far apart. Not often that a young person meets anybody their age. You'll be welcome every Sunday while you're stayin' with Len. Usually a lot more people than this. Depends what's happenin' with the seasons. Lots more visitin' in the winter if there ain't too much snow.

A wind blowing apples off the trees.
A hand coming down on a cactus.
A dance in a country schoolhouse.

Thursday August 4 1932 - Friday August 5 1932 - Saturday August 6 1932 - Sunday August 7 1932 - Monday August 8 1932 - Tuesday August 9 1932.

What are the Great Divides in your life?
What are the breaks that have occurred?
Are these breaks that last forever or quickly mend?

"The boys and girls grew up and got jobs and brought the money home to put on the kitchen table."

Lytton - Keefers - North Bend - Spuzzum - Haig - Agassiz - Harrison Mills - Mission - Hammond - Westminster Junction - Port Moody - Coquitlam - Vancouver - New Westminster - Coquitlam - Port Moody - Westminster Junction - Hammond.

A black cloud rolling across the landscape.
A hundred hoboes perched on the roof of a boxcar.
A boy with a sign that says will-work-for-food.

Out looking for the line-rider. Twelve or fourteen miles across the prairie. The Cartwrights told us all about him. A ranch of about five thousand acres. Works for the QX ranch. One of the biggest cattle ranches in the West. He rides along the fences. Gone for weeks at a time. Takes two horses or maybe three. All his provisions in saddle-bags. Sleeps right under the stars. If there's a break in the fence, he'll fix it right then and there. That's all he ever does. The rest of us are farmers. A man with a job like his is one of the last true cowboys in the West. So we ride the fourteen miles and what seems like more. Looking for the trail that we were told we couldn't miss. Never seeing a human being or any livestock. Just the prairie and the sky. Darkness comes up quickly here. Finally, we figure we'd better give up and head back to Len's.

Arose at six o'clock and set off in the general direction of the homestead we were looking for. Passing thru chaparral (clumps of bushes) we came upon many bands of cattle. They would rise to their feet move uneasily about and eye us in alarm. A man on foot was to them a

"The more information which each weather station collects, the more information the meteorologist will have in his attempt to predict larger weather patterns."

"Twenty-seven percent of Canadian workers are unemployed."

The boy watches as his father crosses the creek. He walks across the log and jumps down onto the bank. Long strides as he climbs the hill. The same path as the kids all use when they go down to the creek and float their wooden boats. The lunch-pail dangles from his hand. He wears a railroad cap and overalls.

Fragments were scattered - all his provisions - the prairie and the sky - darkness comes up quickly - the synoptic hour - a great deal of information - you're starting fresh - scrubbing a floor - everything covered in dust - a letter to whomever.

Every time you leave the railroad, you lose your seniority. Every time you go away you're starting fresh. Start in as a labourer and work your way up again.

So you laze around St. Thomas, waiting for someone to be sick or injured. Spend an afternoon at the pond or down at the lake.

I help my mother as much as I can. But no one wants you in their home. You start to think you'd be less of a burden if you up and left.

Your mother kneels somewhere
on her knees
scrubbing a floor.

Coming down into a slough. A little lost as far as directions. Seeing a cabin and stopping to ask where we are. Pretty tiny. Just one room. No lock on the door and no sign of anybody living here. Old stove propped up on one leg. A bunk and a table and a chair. Everything covered in dust. A suitcase with some letters and a few stray notes. A letter to whomever finds themselves here. Pretty interesting stuff. Came out West and homesteaded. Left to go fight in the War. Left everything as it was and off he went. Hopes to come back some day. A little work and this place will prosper. Welcome to live here until I get back. Back by Christmas, I'm told, if everything goes well.

strange creature. However, armed with stout clubs, we passed thru and around the bushes, until we were by the herd. Striking a dim trail, that incidentally was a road allowance, we stuck to it till at last skirting a slough we burst into a clearing and found the people we sought.

"Telescopes have also revealed that the various suns and other heavenly bodies are grouped together in what we now call 'galaxies.'"

He sits at the table in the parlour with the family and some of the hands, moving his fingers down the pages by lantern-light. *"A map can be defined as 'a representation of the earth's surface, or part of it, on a flat surface.'"* The farmer smokes his pipe and speaks to the boy, who looks up from the book. "You know that *World Book,* I find, is a hard old book to read. When you look up 'Cattle', say, and the book says 'See Beef', you've got nowhere to go. Someone else has got the book you think you need."

Sharing an old-time feast.
Finding an empty cabin.

Back by christmas - a dim trail - a hard old book - got nowhere to go - his blood and bone - things you get to do - the top of the map - driving them insane - run 'til exhaustion - drop down dead.

Charlie and me weren't getting much work. Charlie's a fireman and I'm a brakeman. We work on different railroads.

Things are so slow with this Depression. Every month they lay a few off. Two or three days' work a month was all there was.

We were both of us living at home. Both of our parents were paying the bills. So we got talking one day and decided to come out here.

So who are these people and what their voices?
Those who bred his blood and bone from ancient times?
Are there some among these folk who bear his name?

Mucking out the barn. Len Yarwood telling his tale as we fork the manure. So I came out here from England and got me a job. I was happy on the Anderson farm, back in St. Thomas. Driving the milk wagon into town and back. All the things you get to do when you work on a farm. The Andersons were good people to work for. You fellows can vouch for that. Always knew I was going to get paid for every day. Steadier work than I'd had back home. Then my brother comes out from England. The older brother and all. Says, Why not go out to Alberta? Way up north at the top of the map. Get us some of this homestead land. A little place called Vermillion. Get us both adjoining sections and work as a team. Well, I felt a little leery – it's a pretty big chance to take – but my brother was pretty convincing – and here we are!

4:56 - 4:57 - 4:58 - 4:59 - 5:00 - 5:01 - 5:02 - 5:03 - 5:04 - 5:05 - 5:06 - 5:07 - 5:08 - 5:09 - 5:10 - 5:11 - 5:12 - 5:13 - 5:14 - 5:15 - 5:16 - 5:17 - 5:18 - 5:19 - 5:20 - 5:21 - 5:22 - 5:23 - 5:24 - 5:25 - 5:26 - 5:27 - 5:28 - 5:29 - 5:30 - 5:31- 5:32 - 5:33 - 5:34 - 5:35 - 5:36 - 5:37 - 5:38.

People
talking
in a house.

An expert predicting future weather.
Sliding a block of ice up a wooden slope.
An old man with a thick Cumberland accent.

People
spilling out
onto a porch.

Who or what has made breaks in your journey?
Have they been self-imposed at all?
Has this been done with a pencil or with a knife?

People carrying
a coffin out
to the street.

    Cutting prairie wool in the sloughs. Having to stop every so often and adjust the cutting knife. Starting the discing with a four-horse team. Hard to keep them all in line. Horses bobbing their heads from the flies. Almost driving them insane. Adjusting the screen muzzle that Len put on to keep the flies from getting inside. The flies are frantic for the moisture in the nose. Don't know what the wild horses do. Heard that moose will run 'til exhaustion and drop down dead.

Chapter 9

Going out after supper and working with Len in the yard. Mending a latch that keeps coming loose on the gate. It's a beautiful crop they tell me. Everybody around here is saying it's going to be such a good year. That there's been no crop like this since '25. Well, it'll put us a little ahead. Buy a few things we need and save the rest. Be nice if these crops keep coming like this but there's bound to be a year, sometime in the future, when the yield is a little thin. Hard to sleep some nights with worry. Still, I'm ever so glad I made the move out here.

Horse almost crazy.

A young fellow wearing a white Stetson.
A boy running beside a train to hitch a ride.
An unlocked door and a warm stove.

Mistaken for rustlers.

Weeds growing up around a plough.
A politician giving a speech on the radio.
Drops of rain on a family album in an empty room.

Thrown clean for my pains.

How would you like to live in Alberta?
Get yourself a section of land?
Building fences, training colts, riding the range?

5:39 - 5:40 - 5:41- 5:42 - 5:43 - 5:44 - 5:45 - 5:46 - 5:47 - 5:48 - 5:49 - 5:50 - 5:51- 5:52 - 5:53 - 5:54 - 5:55 - 5:56 - 5:57 - 5:58 - 5:59 - 6:00 - 6:01 - 6:02 - 6:03 - 6:04 - 6:05 - 6:06 - 6:07 - 6:08 - 6:09 - 6:10 - 6:11 - 6:12 - 6:13 - 6:14 - 6:15 - 6:16 - 6:17 - 6:18 - 6:19.

Riding out to get horses for Len. Grazing with the common herd. Just separate the white mare and get her moving back here and the rest will follow. Sure enough, they all come with us. A group of twenty or so. Riding along and feeling like cowboys with our herd. Suddenly there's a shot! A crash like a falling tree! A cowboy coming towards us! Full gallop on his horse! We stop and wonder what he's going to do. Riding up and cutting us off and starting to shout! What the hell do you think you're doin'? What are you takin' these horses for! Wild eyes and waving his rifle! Just like in the films. These horses are for Yarwood! We're out here visiting Len! He sent us out to bring his horses back! He settles down and explains. There's been rustlin' goin' on! I seen you drivin' these horses! Figured you might put up a fight! You're both of you lucky I didn't let fly at you two!

Rode to Cartwright's had dinner. Rode bareback to Hobsiss, borrowed a saddle, Little girl and I "piled" by horse jumping trail. Played baseball at the school.

"Even deeper below the earth's crust is a core which is believed to be made of such heavy elements as iron and nickel."

And then this boy had come along. The Ontario boy who works with Tom at the Culham farm. And in frustration he had asked the boy, "Does Tom have any beef? Tell him I'll trade this bloody binder for a couple of calves." And so Tom had hurried over from the Culham place. Brought the tractor and these two calves. Never offered to fix the binder. I knew the deal was bad when I shook Tom's hand, but I knew I'd never be able to fix it by myself.

"In Canada, there is an over-supply of pulp and paper and wheat."

Mending a latch - keeps coming loose - such a good year - a little ahead - bound to be a year - hard to sleep - the yield is a little thin - horse almost crazy - thrown clean - both of you lucky.

So I'm a brakeman on the railroad. Worked my way up through the ranks, you might say. My job is to help make up the trains before they leave the yard.
And I was up on top of a boxcar. We were shunting in the yard. That's where you're putting cars together to make a train.
They get the cars all moving pretty fast. And your job is to know when to put on the brakes. The brakes are operated by a brake-wheel on the roof at the end of each car.

Chances are
you'll dig

and find great riches.

Seeking the line-rider again. Riding together across the prairie – Charlie and me. Riding on horseback for miles and miles. Better directions from the Cartwright's neighbours this time. Old time settlers who really know their way around. Finally, we ride right into his camp. One mention of the Cartwrights and all is well. Invited to join him for grub. See that the horses are looked after first! Little oven in front of a fireplace. Making biscuits as he talks. The sourdough sizzles on the pan as he tells us of his job. Rides the fences every day. Seven horses on a string. Hundreds of horses on the ranch and five thousand cattle. The sourdough biscuits are pretty dry but the coffee's good. After lunch we ride alongside him for a couple of miles. In a week or two he'll be back here on the spot. If it's Sunday, he'll visit the Cartwrights for the music and the people and the food.

Back tracked to look for letters, no luck, sharpened mower knife. Went for a ride, broke stirrup leather, horse almost crazy with horse flies and nose flies. Got mistaken for rustlers by wild eyed hombre. Had turned his cow into open range; our mistake.

"*It can also be imagined that if one were to change the location of the light within the glass sphere, one would get differing distortions on the piece of flat paper on which the light is being projected.*"

Admiring a beautiful crop.
Being mistaken for a rustler.

Perhaps if these were different times. Perhaps some emperor eager to pay. Some king – way back in the mists of the olden-time. "Take this bag of gold for your rings. They are intricate; they are exquisite; they are sublime. I shall give one to every ladie at the banquet tonight."

The core of the earth - to fix the binder - the deal was bad - I'd never be able - make up the trains - putting cars together - your job is to know - all is well - ride alongside him - the music and the people and the food.

So we're going pretty fast along the tracks. And I'm standing on the roof of one of the boxcars. And they'll crash if I don't slow things down for the coupling of the cars.
So I put my stick in the brake-wheel. And suddenly, she snapped! And it threw me backward and I fell and twisted my leg.
Well, it gave me quite a jolt. Threw me right down on the ground. If I'd fallen a different way, I'd have been down underneath those train-wheels and that would be that.

"Did you bring a truth with you?" asked the tree.

Coming back across the prairie. Miles from anywhere and riding along. My horse is slower than Charlie's. Falling back and catching up. Skirting around a slough. A bunch of cattle here for the water. Next thing I know, I'm flat out on the ground! Calling out for Charlie! Hustling over to a clump of trees! All these cattle closing in on me! Can't read anything in their eyes! No idea if they'll attack or let me go! Charlie coming back at a gallop! Leading my horse by the reins! The cattle all scatter aside! Don't feel safe until I get back up on my horse!

A countryside ravaged by a grasshopper plague.
A carpenter levelling the wall-plate of a house.
A farmer looking over his section of land.

Wednesday August 10 1932 - Thursday August 11 1932 - Friday August 12 1932 - Saturday August 13 1932 - Sunday August 14 1932 - Monday August 15 1932 - Tuesday August 16 1932.

A line-rider, mending miles of fences?
All your possessions in a couple of saddle bags?
Sourdough biscuits sizzling over an open fire?

"And the boy dropped out of school and delivered groceries all over town with a horse and a wagon."

Mission - Harrison Mills - Agassiz - Haig - Spuzzum - North Bend - Keefers - Lytton - Spencer Bridge - Ashcroft - Savour - Tranquille - Kamloops - Pritchard - Shuswai - Salmon Arm - Sicanmous - Craigellachie.

A faint train whistle in the night.
A woman washing laundry in a tub.
A storekeeper sweeping his sidewalk.

Up early every morning. Four or five o'clock. Tending the livestock and other chores before we have breakfast. Helping Len with whatever needs doing. Plenty of jobs around the place. Bringing horses in from the range. Helping to disc the breaking. Washing clothes when we get some time. Charlie sick with too much sun. Making a swing for Len's brother's baby. Sharpening saws and grinding the tools that hang in the shed.

Cut prairie wool, fixed mower knife. Started discing, four horses. Len found letters intact.

"Of course, with weather changing rapidly, it is important to send the information to a central location immediately."

"Two hundred thousand farmers in Saskatchewan are on relief."

Idle chatter around the table as they eat. What was said and what was sung this morning in church. What to do this afternoon? Where to go and who to see? Doesn't look like there'll be any chance of rain.

Great variety of projections - the location of the light - if these were different times - underneath those train-wheels - can't read anything - bring a truth with you - whatever needs doing - to be of any use - been through it before - looked among the flowers.

Must have been pretty hard for my mom. Because she'd been through it before. Now here's her son brought home from an accident at the railroad yards.
Great big bandage on my foot. Pair of crutches from the hospital. Those fellows from the roundhouse didn't leave 'til they knew I was settled down.
Anyways, she didn't get too upset. Brought a pillow and some blankets to the front verandah. Put the kettle on and made a cup of tea.

They looked in the grass and they looked among the flowers.
They looked near the gnome and far away.

Len mending a broken harness. Cutting a piece of leather. Punching holes to make a strap. Took me a while to agree with my brother, but here I am. There's no more land, you know, in England. Even Ontario's getting the same. Just think – if I'd have stayed back in St. Thomas, I'd be working in Anderson's fields. The crop wouldn't be my own. And it wouldn't be six hundred acres – that's for sure. Drawing someone else's paycheque on someone else's land – not like it is here. Things are good out here in Canada. All these acres belong to me. Every so often I write back to England and give them the news.

Rode 7 miles to the line riders had supper there (John McKinley) Range consisted of 8 sections 32 miles around. 1000 cattle 110 horses. Licked stubborn horse, got thrown clean for my pains. surrounded by wild eyed steers; bad situation; Charlie caught horse.

"There are an unknown number of galaxies of all shapes and sizes, perhaps measuring in the billions."

Finally, the two boys reach the top of Sulphur Mountain. Six hours since they set out on their climb from Banff. Two and a half hours of slipping and sliding on the face. A cold and clammy wind. Mosquitoes in clouds. They look out over the valley at Banff below. Soaked in sweat at eight thousand feet. Too exhausted to even think of sliding back down. They shuffle through the loose shale and rock of the summit and enter the observatory. They stand in line to register their names.

    Mucking out the barn.
    Riding under the Northern Lights.

Give them the news - billions of these galaxies - assume definite shapes - register their names - healed up pretty good - self became the self - better take those coats - soaks up its share - a burst of colour - what the horses are thinking.

So, a week or so on the verandah. My mother bringing me cups of tea. Me saying don't bother too much about me – you've got plenty to do.

The ankle healed up pretty good. I'm okay for getting around. I can do my job as well as any man.

Just can't walk as far as I need to. On this trip we've had to make some pretty big hikes. The ankle breaks out in pain, sometimes, and I have to rest, and then, after a while, I'm okay.

His dreams became the dreams,
His nightmares became the nightmares,
His self became the self of the puppeteer.

Every place here is far away. Five miles to see Len's girlfriend and her parents. Ten or eleven miles to get horses. The line rider's circuit, he told us, is thirty-two miles around. We ride fourteen miles for a ball game and a dance and then back again. Hot weather in the daytime, but Len says to take the heavy coats. You might be sweating while playing baseball, but you'll be freezing while riding home. I'm telling you, you better take those coats!

5:39 - 5:40 - 5:41- 5:42 - 5:43 - 5:44 - 5:45 - 5:46 - 5:47 - 5:48 - 5:49 - 5:50 - 5:51- 5:52 - 5:53 - 5:54 - 5:55 - 5:56 - 5:57 - 5:58 - 5:59 - 6:00 - 6:01 - 6:02 - 6:03 - 6:04 - 6:05 - 6:06 - 6:07 - 6:08 - 6:09 - 6:10 - 6:11 - 6:12 - 6:13 - 6:14 - 6:15 - 6:16 - 6:17 - 6:18 - 6:19.

A rose
blooms
in the sunshine.

Huddling under a tarpaulin in slashing rain.
A pen moving slowly across a page.
A woman making notes for a book.

Its roots
soak up
the moisture.

Riding alone under Western skies?
Coyotes howling at the moon?
A thousand stars and a bedroll on the ground?

A thorn
soaks up its share
of the sun and the rain.

Heading back home to Len's place. Riding home about midnight across the prairie. Glad to have the sheepskin coats. Suddenly a burst of colour! There it is! The Northern Lights! A sight which is out of this world! All the colours of the rainbow meeting in an arch in the middle of the sky! Lighting up the entire countryside as far as the eye can see! We stop the horses and marvel! Cold as the devil, but what a sight! You never see them in Ontario! Colder and colder as we're riding home! All the way home beneath that sky! Such a sight as I never imagined! Absolutely magnificent! Wonder what the horses are thinking as they plod along?

Chapter 10

Staying on at Len's. Helping out as best we can. Making pokes for the cows. Rounding up the work-horses. Finishing the floating. Riding over to the Cartwrights. Drawing in some loads of hay. Taking us longer than we expected. Six loads in the barn by midnight. A five-mile ride to get back to Len's. Exhausted. Letting the horses take us home.

Made pokes for cows.

Two Studebakers in a chicken-shed.
A boy gathering roses from a trellis.
A weather forecast on the radio.

Let horses take us home.

A fisherman casting his line in a stream.
A lady with a child on her hip.
A bricklayer mixing mortar on a board.

Woke up side tracked.

What are tools that no one uses?
A concertina that no one can play?
What are letters in the attic that no one reads?

6:20 - 6:21 - 6:22 - 6:23 - 6:24 - 6:25 - 6:26 - 6:27 - 6:28 - 6:29 - 6:30 - 6:31- 6:32 - 6:33 - 6:34 - 6:35 - 6:36 - 6:37 - 6:38 - 6:39 - 6:40 - 6:41- 6:42 - 6:43 - 6:44 - 6:45 - 6:46 - 6:47 - 6:48 - 6:49 - 6:50 - 6:51- 6:52 - 6:53 - 6:54 - 6:55 - 6:56 - 6:57 - 6:58 - 6:59 - 7:00 - 7:01 - 7:02.

A Sunday spent at the Cartwights'. Another one of those Western feasts. Me and Charlie helping out. A basement like a cold-cellar. Jars and jars and jars. Every kind of food you'd want. The fiddle playing while we help

Mrs. Cartwright collect her jars. All the food she'll need to make the evening feast. Oh everyone comes here, she says. They know they're always welcome. They don't need an invitation. There's about twenty out there now. Cowboys, stock ranchers, sheep herders. Those two brothers who herd the sheep – we're the only people they know. We don't see them for weeks at a time, but then a Sunday will roll around and here they are. The line-rider comes about two or three times in a year.

Bring horses from the range each morning. washed clothes; helped disc the breaking. Charlie sick; too much sun. Made swing for baby. Rode 5 miles to ball game and dance. Had good time, Horse tried to buck me off. I got the decision this time.

"The earth's surface is surrounded by a number of envelopes which consist of liquids and gases."

We had so much money in those days – '25 and '26. Dollars comin' out of our ears. Record yields and record prices. Wheat was money – money was wheat. Now I've got two cars and no one to sell them to.

"Argentina, Australia and the Soviet Union are all dumping surplus wheat on the world markets."

Six loads in the barn - making pokes for cows - jars and jars and jars - cowboys, stock ranchers, sheep herders - disc the breaking - know the great divide - every drop of water - riding like gang-busters - smooth as you please - not like in the movies.

Do you know the Great Divide? Where the waters part in the mountains? I think I dream about it all the time.
Just another day in my life. Getting off and looking around. Reading the sign that says the waters flow from here.
Eating a sandwich and taking a drink. Sitting on top of the world in a way. Every drop of water flows somewhere from here.

The seeds will stir in the warm moist ground.
More than I can believe.

Riding five miles for a game and a dance. Playing baseball at the school. Looking up at the strangest thing. A guy on a horse riding like gang-busters over the hill. Riding as fast as a regular cowboy. With his leg sticking straight out in front. Got his leg in a plaster cast. Swinging down out of that saddle just as smooth as you please. A horse-breaker, someone says. Fell off a horse and broke his leg. From his toes right up to the hip in a plaster cast. Can still ride a horse but can't dance or swing at a ball. Not like in the movies. Never see a cowboy in the movies with a broken leg.

Made Pokes for cows, rounded up work horses. finished floating. Rode our ponies to Cartwright's, drew in 6 load of hay, quit at 11:45 pm. Let horses take us home.

"Only at the point where the glass globe touches the paper will the projections be accurate, with distortions increasing with increasing distance between the two."

Sharing a prairie feast.
Playing baseball and attending a dance.

"I see sunshine and I see shadow," says Madame Florina. She looks deep down inside the crystal ball. Outside, the sound of a volleyball game at the beach. "I see that eventually the gloomy shadow will come to pass."

These projections will be correct - the amount of distortion - the periphery of the map - inside the crystal ball - waiting for water - flowers in someone's garden - serves me right - a job on the railroad - while he was alive - the sky the wind and the land.

Just a thought is all it is. How a drop of rain can fall and land on the ground. And wherever it falls, it starts to trickle down.
So there were plants growing there. Lichens and things like that. Things that are waiting for water from there right down to the coasts.
So a drop falls on a mountain. It might grow grass in a mountain valley or flowers in someone's garden. It might even end up in an ocean on either side.

Pour the footings below the frost line.
Take your time to level the wall-plate.

Charlie telling a story at dinner. Went over to see the Norwegian girl. About ten or eleven miles. Invited me for dinner. Wore my nice suit that my mother sent out from home. Tied my horse up at the fence and took my chaps off and walked up to the house. And a couple of young cowboys started to laugh. Must be the city-suit, I thought, as I came up and knocked on the door. Must think I'm from down-town Toronto or something like that! And then she was smiling too, as I walked into the house, so I asked if it was the city-suit that made her laugh. Go over to the mirror and take a look! So I turned my back to the mirror and saw what the laughter was all about. A perfectly-formed brown vee! Everywhere on the suit except where the chaps were! On my pants and on the back of my Sunday coat! It was the oil from that saddle I took from the barn! I had dinner sitting on some grain sacks so I wouldn't ruin her chair! Serves me right for riding a horse in my Sunday-suit!

A heavy volume at the bottom of a backpack.
Two farmhands searching for a lost cow in a wheat field.
A vase lying shattered on the floor.

Wednesday August 17 1932 - Thursday August 18 1932 - Friday August 19 1932 - Saturday August 20 1932 - Sunday August 21 1932 - Monday August 22 1932.

What is a fence that has a hole?
What is lettuce that rabbits steal?
What is a dog that can never catch the thieves?

"And the young man got a job on the railroad and went to work every day as the railroad was always busy while he was alive."

Taft - Revelstoke - Kicking Horse Pass - Connaught Tunnel - Beavermouth - Donald - Golden - Field - Lake Louise - Banff - Sulphur Mountain - Morley - Cochrane - Calgary - Airdrie - Crossfield - Carstairs - Olds - Forth.

A group of protesters hoisting we-want-work signs.
Repossession agents knocking on a door.
Wind howling round a deserted shack.

Taking two horses out for a run. Charlie and me like cowboys. Just the sky the wind and the land. Following the buffalo trails. Running across the prairie and through the hills. No more than three or four feet wide. Down a foot or so. Worn into the ground. Where they had their dust baths and their mud baths at the edges of the sloughs. Moving up into the rocks. A channel as smooth as glass. Round and round the rubbing stone. Hard to believe there used to be thousands of buffalo here.

Rode horses 2 miles to return saddle, came back bareback. Made up our packs, had dinner at Yarwood's and walked 5 miles to Cartwright's. Rainstorm kept us from seeing the line rider. Helped with chores and cowboy came in to play the fiddle. Had a sing song till 12 pm.

"*The centrally-located meteorologist works as quickly as possible to use the information from the weather stations before it becomes obsolete.*"

"Fifteen percent of all Canadians are on relief."

The man opens the little box. The candle shines on the concertina. Two leather belts around his fingers. His fingers splayed on the little keys. He pulls it apart and squeezes it in. So fast it's as if the fingers fly. Everybody raises a glass of the good stuff. The people sing and tap their feet. A tune with the lilt of home so far away.

The rubbing stone - shines on the concertina - might not seem like much - isn't much to do there - engineer sounds the signal - cool draught of water - beautiful crop to look at - a long ways from the barn - can't afford to pay - woke up side tracked.

So it's just a little stream. A little stream about two feet wide. You get off the train and there's the Great Divide.
And it might not seem like much. But it goes to the Atlantic and the Pacific. So narrow, you see, that it's easy to step across.
There isn't much to do there. Just sit on a rock and look around. When the engineer sounds the signal, you get back on the train.

Wisdom roars in gorges,
sweeping everything away.

Saying goodby to Len Yarwood. A cool draught of water beside the pump. Looking out over Len's fields of waving wheat. Waiting for his brother to come and see us before we head out. Hate to see you two fellows go. It's been a pleasure working with you. When you wrote, I remembered those days on the Anderson farm. It's a beautiful crop to look at, but it's still a long ways from the barn. I'm out of cash and I don't want to go into debt. Sorry I can't afford to pay you. I know you can't work for free. I could use the help, but I can't afford to pay.

Travelling very slow on a local freight. had a diner on train, baloney, bread butter raspberry jam. Arrived at North Battleford at 7 pm. Washed up at power house left at 10 P.M. Rode coal car as per last night, Woke up side tracked at the right place.

"Our own galaxy, which includes our planets and our sun, appears to be arranged in the shape of a disc."

A red-letter day today. The colts are broken to the cart. They perform like a couple of old horses. He drives them at least two miles down the dirt road and back. Getting them used to the tug of the harness. Getting them used to the reins on their backs. Getting them used to the 'chuck' to start and the 'whoa' to stop. Later he turns them out in the yard and watches as they frisk like puppies again.

>Following the buffalo trails.
>Saying goodbye to a friend.

At the right place - our own star - a red-letter day - reins on their backs - frisk like puppies - picture of myself - up in heaven - something I have to do - it slides back off - never seen so much hay.

So let me tell you about my dream. I see this picture of myself. There I am on one side of the Great Divide.

So I know that I'm up in heaven. I see two angels coming down. Two angels coming down on a slant on either side.

It's all black behind in the sky. These angels are pure white and with great big wings. And they come down almost to the ground and they beckon to me.

And I say, "I can't go yet – there's something I have to do." It seems like forever as the angels flap their wings. And then they turn and they go way back up in the sky.

The miller mills the flour in the stone.
What he is and what he does is his gift.

Catching an Eastbound freight. Jumping a boxcar full of coal. Making beds of straw and paper. Overalls rolled up for a pillow. Settling down and having a sleep. Two days on slow-moving freights. Dinner of baloney, bread, butter and raspberry jam. All the stuff that Mrs. Cartwright put in our packs. Leaving Alberta and on to Saskatchewan. North Battleford, Keniston, Saskatoon. Walking for fourteen miles. Meal for a quarter. Shower at the Y. Fifty miles from Aylesbury. Six cents for a dozen eggs. A temporary job on a farm. A couple days' work and then we'll walk to the Culham place.

6:20 - 6:21 - 6:22 - 6:23 - 6:24 - 6:25 - 6:26 - 6:27 - 6:28 - 6:29 - 6:30 - 6:31- 6:32 - 6:33 - 6:34 - 6:35 - 6:36 - 6:37 - 6:38 - 6:39 - 6:40 - 6:41- 6:42 - 6:43 - 6:44 - 6:45 - 6:46 - 6:47 - 6:48 - 6:49 - 6:50 - 6:51- 6:52 - 6:53 - 6:54 - 6:55 - 6:56 - 6:57 - 6:58 - 6:59 - 7:00 - 7:01 - 7:02.

A photograph
on the wall
above a fireplace.

A lady looking into a crystal ball.
A dog sniffing around a hole in a fence.
A pot of stew which never seems to boil.

*A young man
with a
handlebar moustache.*

A verandah on which people die?
An old house that is falling down?
What are roses on a trellis surrounded by thorns?

*Dressed up
in a Sunday-suit
and an old-fashion tie.*

Cutting hay all day in Saskatchewan. Didn't take long to find us some work. Working for a man named Packard. Each with a team and a mowing machine. Breaking a blade and getting it fixed. Then at it with vengeance again. Round and round inside a big slough. Making a game of it to see who cuts the most. Pretty slippery stuff. More like grass than it is like hay. You fork it on the wagon and it slides back off. We are nothing if not persistent. Mr. Packard is certainly pleased. You boys is pretty good workers! In all these years I never seen so much hay!

Chapter 11

Taken on by the Culham's. Ainsley and May, Ivan and Orla. Father, mother, son and little girl. And a hired man named Tom, who looks after the teams. It's a pretty good set-up here. Twelve hundred acres of land and a real nice spread. Three full meals and all you can eat. A bedroom right in the house for Charlie and me. Looks like it's going to be all right. Two dollars a day and bed and board, though all you get is your meals on a day that it rains. That's fair enough, I'd say. We heard some terrible stories from guys on the trains about how you get treated on some of the farms. We're lucky they're taking us on. All Charlie doesn't like is the constant wind.

Improved my knowledge.

A shelf filled with jars and jars of food.
Flowers swaying in the back seat of a car.
A drop of rain falling on the ground.

Feet getting tender.

A begging bowl with pennies on the sidewalk.
A jailor handing out meal-chits.
A farmer asking a banker for a loan.

An appalling black cloud.

Why not spend your life in Saskatchewan?
Acres and acres of waving wheat?
Bring in young fellows from Ontario at harvest time?

7:03 - 7:04 - 7:05 - 7:06 - 7:07 - 7:08 - 7:09 - 7:10 - 7:11 - 7:12 - 7:13 - 7:14 - 7:15 - 7:16 - 7:17 - 7:18 - 7:19 - 7:20 - 7:21 - 7:22 - 7:23 - 7:24 - 7:25 - 7:26 - 7:27 - 7:28 - 7:29 - 7:30 - 7:31- 7:32 - 7:33 - 7:34 - 7:35 - 7:36 - 7:37 - 7:38 - 7:39 - 7:40 - 7:41- 7:42 - 7:43 - 7:44.

Starting right in to work. Up before dawn and washing up at the pump. Tending to the livestock and wolfing breakfast down and out to the fields. Drawing hay to the barn and building up a stack. Pretty much what we did in St. Thomas on the Anderson farm. Pitching hay with a fork tightens up the old arms, so soon we'll be in shape. Hot as Hades in the barn, but a nice breeze on the way back and forth from the fields. Supper's tasting pretty good at the end of the day. Oh, wait – the day's not over yet. We work after supper as well. Loading a cow on a wagon and going three miles at a trot. Mr. Culham trading for another cow and bringing it back.

Drew hay to barn and built a stack. After supper loaded cow into wagon and drove 3 miles at a trot. brought a cow back, which got out twice, and we rounded it up on horseback. But what a roundup! Thru wheat as high as our heads.

"Water accounts for seventy-one percent of the earth's visible surface while land accounts for twenty-nine percent of the surface of the globe."

A patch of welcoming ground! Nice black, fertile soil! I pick up a clod in my hand and it crumbles nicely! Sandy loam with a hint of clay! Nicely tilled and ready to plant! About thirty by twenty I'd say! About the size to feed a family! Surrounded by lush vegetation! Somebody's property right next door! All kinds of things growing there! Wonder who has claim to all that? At least I've got what I need! What a beautiful piece of property! Everything here to make things grow! Can't help picking up a handful and rubbing it ever so gently between my palms and enjoying the feel!

"The low prices for beef and grains are setting records here in Canada."

Some terrible stories - the constant wind - improved my knowledge - an appalling black cloud - hot as hades - a nice breeze - cover the entire surface - ready to plant - what i need - always play your request.

So what do I have to do?

Well, when I get home, I'll fix the fence. I promised my mom I'd do that this summer, but me and Charlie left town before I got it done. She keeps a garden and the rabbits all have a feast.

And we'll show young Ivan around. He has relatives in Ontario, but he's never been there himself. Take him over to Detroit, then Toronto and Niagara Falls.

There's a band at the Royal York that comes from St. Thomas. If you're from St. Thomas, they'll always play your request. And anything else that Ivan would like to see.

The road is much steeper
now the donkey's dead.

Searching for a lost cow in a wheat field. Charlie and me calling out as we wander around. Don't get lost or we'll have to look for both you and the cow! Wheat as high as our heads. Like wandering around in a labyrinth. Like those ancient kings used to do. Footprints here and there. Wheat-stocks broken down, but where did she go? These fields go on for miles. Wouldn't want for us to get lost. Charlie's voice is getting fainter. Hey Charlie, let's stick close together! We better figure out a plan! How do you go about finding a cow in a thousand-acre wheat-field? Better find her soon and get her back to the barn! From now on, we better tie those knots real tight!

Quite day, done our washing. Improved my knowledge by reading World books.

"It follows then that the lines which are at the centre of both the glass sphere and the flat paper will yield an accurate comparison."

Moving in with a family.
Working in the fields.

Planting the seeds in the ground! Taking the stipple and making a mark! Sighting along the rows to make sure she's square! Putting one seed in every hole! Covering up each seed and packing the soil! Tamping it down with a gentle touch! Leaving just a dent to help collect the rain! This has to be the most beautiful soil! Just to hold some in my hands is a perfect joy! Filling the bucket at the well! Just a splash or two for now for every seed! This neighbouring property sure is lush! Abundance right up to the fence! Looks good for the seeds I'm planting on my patch of soil!

Road is much steeper - in a labyrinth - stick close together - figure out a plan - improved my knowledge - considered as being true - the most beautiful soil - the seeds i'm planting - absorbed in what i'm doing - looks like a pearl.

I love to work at carpentry work. I get so absorbed in what I'd doing, I forget to eat. Never think about whether I've had my dinner or not.
I like the smell of the wood. I like how it handles. I think there's nothing like a nice, straight, clean board that's been well-planed.
I just love to work with wood. What I love best, I'd say, is the grain on a piece of white oak. When I sand it down, it looks like a pearl to me.

Most of the pieces were quickly found.
But there was one piece that had completely disappeared.

Up at 5:00 a.m. Hitch up the hay racks and on the road at 7:00 a.m. Driving ten miles and then raking and stacking hay. Collecting it all from the sloughs. Very hot in hilly country. Not a whisper of a breeze. A cold dinner in the shade of the wagon in the heat of noon. Cold pork, pickles and water. Plenty of Saskatoon berries too. A couple of pailfuls for dessert. Cooling off as the day winds down. Working as late as we can see. Cooking our supper by firelight before we head home.

A boy walking along with a pack on his back.
A fork-full of grass sliding off a wagon.
A stone pressing downward on a chest.

Tuesday August 23 1932 - Wednesday August 24 1932 - Thursday August 25 1932 - Friday August 26 1932 - Saturday August 27 1932 - Sunday August 28 1932 - Monday August 29 1932.

Put down roots in the prairie soil?
Look around for a suitable wife?
Beget children you could mention in your will?

"And one day the young man got married in the church with his family all there and rice was thrown and the two went off on their honeymoon."

Red Deer - Lacombe - Ponoka - Wetaskin - Leduc - Edmonton - Vegreville - Vermillion - Hobsiss - Lloydminster - Battle River - Marsden - Balinora - Baldwin - Cut Knife - North Battlefield - Battleford - Rockhaven - Thackery.

A locomotive puffing up a grade.
A brother and sister playing checkers beside the fire.
A line of laundry hanging on a line.

Up again at 5:00 a.m. Hearty breakfast and out again to work on the hay. Building stacks as we cut in the sloughs. Loading the wagon after dinner for a trip to town. Heat is terrific out here in the West. Ten miles to town on the wagon. Having our supper on the way. Horses' feet getting tender. Not getting back to the barn until 9:00 p.m.

Up at 5 a.m.; rough breakfast, back to hay; built stacks in each slough. Loaded wagons for town after dinner, heat terrific. Ten miles to town, had supper on the way, Horses feet getting tender. Got thru at 9 p.m.

"The information from each weather station is plotted onto a large map which records the weather from the entire area of concern."

"There are Canadians who would rather starve than go on relief."

Filling the bucket at the well! Sure we've had our share of rain, but I want to be sure! Pouring just the right amount over every seed! This soil just seems so lush! The perfect place for planting seeds! Wonder who owns that place over there? How long ago did they plant? Wonder what kinds of plants those are? All that lush vegetation, but I can't see fruit from here! Wonder what they get when they harvest? Must be loaded down with their yield! Anyways, things are going well here! Just the right amount of rain and lots of sunshine! Don't want to overdo the watering! Don't want the seeds to rot! Hard to just let things take their course! Hard to look each day and not see anything peeking through! They talk about watching a kettle, but with seeds you can't even watch them as they grow!

Each piece of information - our share of rain - the perfect place - all that lush vegetation - things take their course - all my father's tools - a fledgling boy - starting to worry a bit - a chilly blast - left destitute by hail.

I have all my father's tools. Some came all the way from England. Some of them could be a hundred years old.

Planes and saws and a drill and a drawknife – all in a box he made himself. I've got it in the room where me and Ken sleep. I've got every tool a carpenter would ever need.

You've heard of Sheffield steel? That's a city in England where they make the very best steel. Some of the tools say 'Sheffield Steel' stamped on the side.

But what I'd like best is to be a railroad carpenter. They go everywhere the railroad goes and work with everything wood. Repair old buildings and build new buildings too.

And you are flying everywhere
on the wings
of a fledgeling boy.

Looking up from a *World Book* article. Charlie polishing his knife. You know, I think we're gonna do all right out of this. Two dollars a day except if it rains. We cleaned the granary out today to get ready for the threshing. Mr. Culham says we'll have work every day 'til the end of September. You stook for a mile, he says, and there's another mile to go. And after that there's still another mile. Seven hundred acres before we're done. All that travel was really interesting, but I was starting to worry a bit. Helping Len was great but he couldn't afford to pay. Hate to spend the summer working and nothing saved.

We get our first breath of ozone here at 4:45 am. While stooking today, an appalling black cloud swept up from the west, fine silt left the ground in clouds, obscuring the light. A chilly blast followed the storm. Some more farmers left destitute by hail.

"From our vantage point on the earth's surface, we are able to see most of the stars which constitute what might be called 'our home galaxy.'"

She stands beside the stove as she stirs a steaming pot. The soup slowly swirls as she reads. Hi Mom. Things are drying up here at Yarwood's. Len and everybody's been treating us really well and I've been saving all my money – except I bought myself a big hat – so I should have a nest-egg when I get back home. Charlie and me are going to move on to Saskatchewan as we're told there should be lots of work there in the harvest. How's the fence holding up? Did Ken manage to patch it? Is it keeping the rabbits out? Tell the dog to be extra vigilant. Tell him the lettuce is just for us and nobody else. I'll write to you from Saskatchewan when we get there. We'll stay out here as long as the harvest lasts.

Raking and stacking hay.
Baking in the sun.

See most of the stars - should have a nest-egg - be extra vigilant - as long as the harvest lasts - a full day's work - to build a house - come home every day - instead of his name - dreams of rabbits - where the tears ran down.

Hope the railroad picks up steam. They're laying off right now. To get a full day's work every day would be heaven to me.
Some day I'd like to build a house. Tear down my dad's old house and build a new one right next door. Take a course up at Green's Lumber like they advertise you can do.
And then some day a wife and kids. Work on the railroad. Come home every day.

Stalking deer or digging peat or harvesting grain.
Hands rigging sails or shaping wood.
Each one pauses as he works and turns and speaks.

A fellow arrives from Dewdney. Young fellow from Dewdney, BC. Charlie and me are the grizzled veterans. Blisters on our hands – we've been around. Everything he says is 'Dewdney'. They've got everything right there in town. Newspaper office, gas for the cars, bank for your money, school for your kids. Everyone chuckles every time he says the word 'Dewdney'. Everybody starts calling him 'Dewdney' instead of his name.

    7:03 - 7:04 - 7:05 - 7:06 - 7:07 - 7:08 - 7:09 - 7:10 - 7:11 - 7:12 - 7:13 - 7:14 - 7:15 - 7:16 - 7:17 - 7:18 - 7:19 - 7:20 - 7:21 - 7:22 - 7:23 - 7:24 - 7:25 - 7:26 - 7:27 - 7:28 - 7:29 - 7:30 - 7:31- 7:32 - 7:33 - 7:34 - 7:35 - 7:36 - 7:37 - 7:38 - 7:39 - 7:40 - 7:41- 7:42 - 7:43 - 7:44.

A sleeping dog
whimpers
and his feet twitch.

Rain drizzling down from the roof of a porch.
A singsong around an old piano.
A bullet pinging against the side of a train.

He dreams of rabbits
crowding round
the garden gate.

Go back to Ontario every few years?
Won't there be time when the harvest is done?
Enjoy the scenery from the train as you think of the past?

The dog sighs
as the rabbits search
for a hole in the fence.

    Driving a binder with a four-horse team. The team stopping and pulling the binder clear around. Charlie asking me what's going on, but I don't know. Checking the harness to see what's gone wrong. Charlie shouting and pointing at the horizon! A big, black cloud rolling towards us! Grabbing some sheaves and making a pile! The soil coming in like a snow-storm! Every sheaf getting blasted away! Turning our backs and lying down and covering our heads! Icy wind and a curtain of black and then it's gone! Mud on our faces and in our ears. Shirts filled up with pads of mud. Wiping our eyes and checking the horses. Their fur plugged with gumbo and lines down the sides of their faces where the tears ran down.

    A lone man who is far away from home.

    Charlie talking about the West. Late at night, before we put the lantern out. Wouldn't want to live out here. Great people, but the landscape drives me nuts! Where are the trees? Where are the rivers? Where are the valleys? Where are the beaches – those big sandy beaches we have back home! And the wind! The constant wind! I couldn't stand to live out here! Even the apples aren't the same! They talk about the apples out in BC as if they're the best that money can buy, but you can give me an Ontario apple every time!

Chapter 12

On our slow way out to the fields. Stooking starts today. Not looking forward to it, but we came out here to earn money and that's what we'll do. Stories of wearing out leather gloves and fainting from heat stroke in the fields, and fellows quitting after just a few days and going home. Maybe we should have stayed in Alberta. Got ourselves a job on a ranch. Riding the range and fixing fences looks good right now. Leaving my Stetson on the dresser. Wearing our overalls from now on. Could be a month of nothing but stooking in the fields.

Stooking.

Feasting on a find of wild raspberries.
A man on foot amid a herd of menacing cattle.
A puppet gaining control of a puppeteer.

Stooking.

Workers loading freighters at the dock.
A Saturday morning confab in a barber shop.
A girl washing her hair in a metal tub.

Stooking.

So do you like the life of stooking?
Fourteen-hour days in the fields?
Is this what your life is going to be?

7:45 - 7:46 - 7:47 - 7:48 - 7:49 - 7:50 - 7:51- 7:52 - 7:53 - 7:54 - 7:55 - 7:56 - 7:57 -7:58 - 7:59 - 8:00 - 8:01 - 8:02 - 8:03 - 8:04 - 8:05 - 8:06 - 8:07 - 8:08 - 8:09 - 8:10 - 8:11 - 8:12 - 8:13 - 8:14 - 8:15 - 8:16 - 8:17 - 8:18 - 8:19 - 8:20 - 8:21 - 8:22 - 8:23 - 8:24 - 8:25 - 8:26 - 8:27.

Stooking, stooking, stooking. Up at 4:00 a.m. Feeding the horses, gobbling breakfast and out to the fields. Stooking, stooking, stooking. Putting a tick on the corner of the calendar. Monday August 15, 1932. Tuesday, August 16, 1932. Wednesday, August 17, 1932. Thursday, August 18, 1932. Stopping at 9:00 p.m. at night when it's growing too dark to see. Not an ounce of energy left. Back to the barn, take care of the horses, something to eat. Then fall into bed and up at 4:00 a.m.

Stooking.

"Though the atmosphere extends above the earth for two hundred miles, it becomes so thin that most of its density is contained within the first eleven miles."

Money in – money out. Plant the seed and pray to God. Hope the weather holds through the harvest. Be nice to be one of these kids. Come out here from Ontario and work in the fields. Every day they've got a buck and a half in their hands.

"Income from agriculture is down ninety-four percent in the prairie provinces."

Not looking forward - fainting from heat stroke - looks good right now - nothing but stooking - up at 4:00 am - too dark to see - not an ounce of energy - fall into bed - one of these kids - one of us said.

So the work dried up at home. I was a brakeman and Charlie was a fireman on another railroad. We were swimming at Pinafore Park one afternoon.
Used to be lots of work at that ice-house, one of us said. All winter sliding blocks of ice up a wooden ramp. Now it's summer and we just lie in the sun and swim.
Both of us living at home with our folks. Only a few day's pay a month. Putting pennies on the table to help pay the bills.

Chances are
you'll dig
and find just stone.

Stooking, stooking stooking. Gathering up eight sheaves. Two and two and two and two. Standing them up in a shock, all leaning together. Drinking a gallon of water a day. Wearing the fingers out of a pair of thick leather gloves. Working in a field at least a mile long. Stopping for a drink and a stretch for the back. Be back in this field tomorrow and stooking all day again. Seven hundred acres, all waiting for stooking. Seven hundred acres all waiting for me.

Stooking.

"Conversely, if the paper is wrapped around the glass sphere, a cylindrical projection will be obtained."

Stooking in the fields.
Flopping into bed.

Just notes is all it is. Just a jumble of jangling noises. People ask what I'm trying to play and I say I don't know. But if I can play it once, I'll know that I've found my tune.

Sliding blocks of ice - pennies on the table - all leaning together - wearing the fingers out - another group of projections - jumble of jangling noises - I've found my tune - expecting a bumper harvest - what roots did I have.

You know there's work way out in the West. They're expecting a bumper harvest. We should go on the hobo and earn ourselves some cash.
We even knew a man in Alberta. Worked with him on the Anderson farm. Why not go out there and try to find steady work?
Hard to pull myself up by the roots? What roots did I have to pull? People leave home so there will be one less mouth to feed!

"I do not understand," said the woodsman.
He was impatient to put new wisdom into play.
"I have come here seeking truth to add to truth."

Writing 'stooking' in my diary. Just 'stooking' and nothing more. Too tired to write a thing besides the word. Day after day after day. Sleep and eat and work. Two dollars for every day. Bed and board included. Clean the barn on rainy days for just your food. Watch broke on the second day. Have to tell the time by our shadows. Our shadows are moving as slow as they can. When the sun isn't shining, we can't tell time at all. When it's dark we knock off work and head to the barn.

A rider taking a horse up over the jumps.
A diary with all the pages blank.
A young man with a scar on his neck.

Tuesday August 30 1932 - Wednesday August 31 1932 - Thursday Sep-

tember 1 1932 - Friday September 2 1932 - Saturday September 3 1932 - Sunday September 4 1932.

Fingernails breaking on the sheaves?
Thistles pricking your blistered palms?
Bludgeoned for endless hours by the sun?

"And the man tore down his father's house and built one of his own with his own two hands."

Wilkie - Naseby - Perdue - Asquith - Saskatoon - Floral - Blucher - Colonsay - Young - Renoun - Imperial - Stalwart - Liberty - Penzance - Craik - Ayslesbury - Watrous - Easter - Craven - Albatross.

A drunk lying in puke in an alleyway.
A man sleeping under newspapers on a park bench.
A rubber truncheon slashing at a hand.

Heavy mist this morning. Too wet to work, Mr. Culham says. Making a couple of bridles. Leather and binder twine. Trying to break the colts to lead. They cavort like a pair of puppies. Too young to pull a cart. Enjoy your freedom while you can – there's work ahead. Staging our own small rodeo. Taking turns showing off. Leaping on and off a galloping horse without a saddle. Riding two or three at a time and lassoing a fence post. Then the mist clears up and we stook all afternoon.

Stooking.

"*As more and more information is placed on the large map, a picture of the weather emerges, in almost real-time, as it is moving across the landscape.*

"Manufacturers are responding to this Depression by laying off workers and cutting production."

The father swings the lunch-pail down. He puts it on the grass. He picks his little boy up in both his hands. A hug and then he swings him right up and around. A moment to steady the boy on his shoulders and straighten his cap. He bends his knees and grabs the lunch-pail. The two are smiling as they stride across the grass.

New wisdom into play - truth to add to truth - can't tell time at all - built one of his own - the weather situation - last synoptic hour - stride across the grass - bubble of rain - bubble of sunshine - stomach empty, stomach full.

We went all the way out to the Coast and back. Every day was like a bubble. A bubble of rain or a bubble of sunshine – until it burst.

Sleeping in ditches, sleeping in boxcars, sleeping in comfortable beds – stomach empty, stomach full, work or play.

A place to stay for a couple of hours. A place to work for a couple of days. A place to harvest a dollar or two with your blistered hands.

If we don't find the little red ball, thought Jimmy's sister,
I don't know what my little brother is going to do.

Stooking all day. Stooking all day. Stooking all day. Driving the binder during the spell-off at noon. Enjoying it more than I used to do when I first started driving. No more getting eaten alive. Got eaten alive the very first day. Couldn't believe how much salve I had to rub on my neck. Mr. Culham told me to use a binder-whip. Just in time to keep the flies from stripping my carcase. I forgot this here is your first time out in the West! Better tell you guys while you still got skin to save! Just you tie a piece of dark cloth right up high on the whip. That way you won't be bothered by them flies. It'll lure them away from that feast on the back of your neck. Sure enough it works like a charm. Working the binder the rest of the day 'til quitting time.

Stooking.

"Because of the way the heavenly bodies in our galaxy give off light, it has been called 'The Milky Way.'"

He has the *World Book* on his knee. Another day too wet to work and the chores all done. *"The term 'weather' has been defined as 'the changing conditions of the atmosphere that are experienced from day to day.'"* The farmer looks out from the porch as the rain pours down. "You can have them books if you want 'em. Take 'em with you when you go. You're the only one who ever seems to read 'em. All that knowledge just sittin' in them books is wasted on me. Maybe there's somethin' in there that'll do you some good some day."

Reading in the barn.
Training two young colts.

Work or play - harvest a dollar or two - got eaten alive - stripping my carcase - works like a charm - all that knowledge - every seed burrows - going to be you - lose my footing - skim along on the surface.

Actually, I was born right here in Canada. About a year after my parents came over on the boat. Don't know much about England – that's all in the past.

I figure everyone ends up somewhere. Don't think of myself as having roots. I could easily plant myself here or in the East.

Every seed burrows into the ground. None of them worries about trying to locate their 'ancestral roots'. You're going to be you whether you're here or on the moon.

The puppeteer tossed and turned.
The nightmares scorched and tormented
while the dreams enthused and inspired the puppeteer.

Charlie's story about the dance. For the men at the dock where we're unloading sacks of grain. Six of us go to this dance in town. We stop at a garage and Ivan buys us something to drink. A pop bottle filled with whiskey. On the way, we pass the bottle and take a few sips. We get to the dance and things are all right. Fiddlers playing and people dancing. Me and one of the girls are cutting a rug. Then, all of a sudden, I lose my footing! Dancing sideways and hitting a post! Sitting on a chair with my legs all rubber and my stomach on fire! What's going on? Why can't I walk? Why can't I see? Thinking I'll die a couple of thousand miles from home! Turns out the guy at the garage thought we knew – that was pure whiskey in that bottle! Wheat-whiskey and nothing else – pure alcohol! It hits Ivan a little later. First whiskey he'd ever bought. Both of us lying on the floor as the others all dance beside us and the fiddlers play. A wagon and pony brings us back home when the dance is over. A couple of days of feeling numb and we both come around!

7:45 - 7:46 - 7:47 - 7:48 - 7:49 - 7:50 - 7:51- 7:52 - 7:53 - 7:54 - 7:55 - 7:56 - 7:57 -7:58 - 7:59 - 8:00 - 8:01 - 8:02 - 8:03 - 8:04 - 8:05 - 8:06 - 8:07 - 8:08 - 8:09 - 8:10 - 8:11 - 8:12 - 8:13 - 8:14 - 8:15 - 8:16 - 8:17 - 8:18 - 8:19 - 8:20 - 8:21 - 8:22 - 8:23 - 8:24 - 8:25 - 8:26 - 8:27.

A concertina
on the shelf
of a table.

A mother snipping roses on a verandah.
A freighter weighing anchor for Hong Kong.
A child who is searching for a little red ball.

Sitting quietly
as the days and nights
go by.

Are you numb from exhaustion?
Are you a miner digging coal?
A donkey pulling an overloaded cart?

No one
in the house
knows how to play.

    Up at 4:45 to get the chores done. Off to Watrous for the day. Just like one big family. All of us cramming into the car. Surprised at the size of the buildings. Never swum in salt water before. Charlie and me can hardly believe it. You don't sink down! You just skim along on the surface like a water-bug! Washing the salt off at the tap and then getting a little sun and diving in again. Like diving into a sponge. Not like the water in Lake Erie. Never thinking to close my mouth. Getting out and rinsing the salt-water off my tongue.

Chapter 13

Rigging a gas engine up to an emery wheel. Too wet to work and it looks like rain all day. Taking a sack and off to the kitchen and getting every knife in the drawer and bringing them out and making them all as sharp as they can be. Warning the guys at suppertime that the knives have all been sharpened. Don't want anyone cutting their tongue off in the middle of the meal!

Visitors and turkey dinner.

A warm stove glowing in an empty room.
Rabbits nibbling in a lettuce patch.
A garden with the softest, blackest soil.

Wet morning, heavy day.

A farm wagon half-buried in the silt.
A plate with one potato and a slice of bread.
A hammer tacking up a no-help-wanted sign.

Tried to break the colts.

What are the bubbles that catch your eye?
What is the gift inside each one?
Should you chase them or simply wait for each to burst?

8:28 - 8:29 - 8:30 - 8:31- 8:32 - 8:33 - 8:34 - 8:35 - 8:36 - 8:37 - 8:38 - 8:39 - 8:40 - 8:41- 8:42 - 8:43 - 8:44 - 8:45 - 8:46 - 8:47 - 8:48 - 8:49 - 8:50 - 8:51 - 8:52 - 8:53 - 8:54 - 8:55 - 8:56 - 8:57 - 8:58 - 8:59 - 9:00 - 9:01 - 9:02 - 9:03 - 9:04 - 9:05 - 9:06 - 9:07 - 9:08 - 9:09.

Sunshine and a heavy wind. The whole gang stooking all afternoon. Wind blowing so rough it feels like it's burning my face. Helping Ivan repair the generator. Roars like an airplane now. Flapjacks for supper. We all tuck in pretty good. A pat of butter and a dollop of syrup on top. Playing checkers and cards in the evening. Just a little bit homesick as I read my letter from Ken. All about mom and the dog and the garden and things back home.

Rain today. Took the small rifle and shot pigeons off the barn; Stalked some crows, and got caught in rain. Had visitors and turkey dinner. Hymnal singsong at night.

"Professor Clark has calculated that since the major axis of the earth is 7,926.5 statute miles and the minor axis is 7,809.5 statute miles, the difference between the two is 1,170.0 statute miles."

I knew that Tom knew what he was doing. He took the binder for a couple of calves. He'll probably untwist those canvas straps and have her humming just like a charm. Tom's a fox when it comes to swapping. Bested me this time fair and square. I've crippled my future out of frustration. This land has a way of breaking you down. Next year, no more binder and no more calves. So should I speak to Ainsley Culham – or just let it go?

"The production of iron and steel is in decline."

Warning the guys - to break the colts - stooking all afternoon - a little bit homesick - colonel clarke's calculations - have her humming - crippled my future - breaking you down - just let it go - never feel loneliness.

Sometimes, I think of myself as a loner. An 'individualist', you could say. I could be a Robinson Crusoe easy enough.
I don't really need any company. Never feel loneliness at all. I never feel lost when I'm by myself.
I can work with wood all day. Draw a line with a ruler and pencil. Take the saw and cut her straight along the line.

The plants will ease through the soft black soil.
More than I can believe.

Charlie going to feed the dog. I go with him and take a look. Feeding the bottomless beast. A show that happens every day after breakfast. Whatever the farmhands don't eat all goes to the dog. He waits for Charlie each morning at the door, like he's wearing a watch. A whole big pan full of biscuits. Charlie takes a biscuit and makes a motion to throw. The jaws open up like an alligator. A slow toss and the biscuit disappears right down the throat. A gulp and then the jaws open up again. They call him the coyote-dog because he goes out into the fields and hunts them down. Helping Charlie measure his stride on the summer-ploughed field. An enormous stride whenever he turns on the speed!

Stooked in the morning, rain at noon. I killed a pig after dinner; meat supply exhausted. Hooked tractor on to the granary and drew it out into the field.

"It follows that the cylindrical projection will show more of the earth's surface than will the flat projection."

Tackling a stack of flapjacks.
Feeding the coyote-dog.

The hoboes come and go. The trains move in and the trains move out. He sits on the platform and weaves his rings. A token of love for my ladie's finger. Intricate, exquisite, sublime. You can weave a hundred rings and not sell one.

Straight along the line - the bottomless beast - measure his stride - meat supply exhausted - a token of love - fine with me - money's just something - keep a few bucks - driven out - the map is complete.

And I don't care much about money. Money's just something to buy what you need. And if someone has more than me, that's fine with me.
I give most of what I earn to my mother. Just keep a few bucks for Charlie and me to travel around. You can buy a gallon of gas for nineteen cents.
A place to sleep. Good meals to eat. That's all I need.

Mix the mortar in proportion.
Every brick pointed and clean.

Reading the *World Book*. Only a couple of volumes here. There's some on every farm in these parts. The Robinson family had to leave 'em. Driven out by the last big drought. Left a couple with every family here abouts. Some of the families read 'em and pass 'em 'round. Don't have time for readin' myself, says Mr. Culham, but if you get these totally read, why we can trade for a couple more with someone else.

A word of warning about the flaws in a map.
Newspapers blowing around in Stanley Park.
A rain drop trickling down to the sea.

Monday September 5 1932 - Tuesday September 6 1932 - Wednesday September 7 1932 - Thursday September 8 1932 - Friday September 9 1932 - Saturday September 10 1932 - Sunday September 11 1932.

What are the bubbles that last a lifetime?
What are the rains that never stop falling?
The rays of sunlight that will always continue to shine?

"And the couple had some children – let's say two boys and a girl – and they all lived in the house that the man had built."

Regina - Qu'Appelle - Indian Head - Wolseley - Grenfell - Broadview - Whitewood - Moosimin - Kirkella - Virdon - Oak Lake - Griswold - Kennay - Brandon - Chater - Camp Hughes - Sydney - MacGregor - Portage La Prairie - Rayburn.

A congregation singing hymns in a church.
A cold cellar filled with jars of preserves.
A theatre with posters of a Hollywood film.

Meeting Miss Trevelean. The school teacher. At the dance. Everyone comes for miles around. Telling about the school where Charlie and me spent the nicest warmest, driest night of our whole trip. Taking a turn around the dance floor. Then we help form up a square. Comparing Ontario and Saskatchewan over a glass of lemonade. I invite her to come to the singsong next Sunday afternoon.

Heavy mist this morning, so we staged a small rodeo, leaping on and off a galloping horse with and without saddle; riding two and three at a time etc. Tried to break the colts to lead. Made a couple of bridles; stooked all afternoon. Rushed to a fire, found it was a straw stack.

"A skilled meteorologist relies on a combination of the weather information which is revealed by the almost real-time map and his own experience as to the ways in which weather has been known to behave in the region of concern."

"Some of the provinces are opening labour-camps for the unemployed."

In front of the little cottage. The family arranging themselves in a pose. A neighbour takes the photograph. Be nice to send one home to England. A dad, a mom and five children. In front of their house on Sunday afternoon.

Most significant advantage - more of the earth's surface - examines all the data - what the future holds - where to be - like the newspapers - loves these horses - had a good time - relatively few number of stars - along the short axis.

Just wonder what the future holds – that's all. This Depression can't last forever. That's what everybody says as we travel around.

Things'll pick up again. Be able to choose a little more. Where to work, where to live, where to be.

Right now we're just knocking around. Wherever there's work, wherever there's pay, wherever there's food. Like the newspapers blowing around in Stanley Park.

Wisdom pools in terraces
where peasants hoe the corn.

Half-sleeping on the wagon as we jog along the path. A lantern on a pole is the only light. Three miles to go before we get to the site today. Tom, the old fellow, telling me all about his team. Loves these horses as if they're his own. Six teams in the field and two for hauling grain. Charlie on a wagon a few teams back. Everything covered in dew. Boots and pant-legs will get soaking-wet as soon as we start to work. They'll dry out when the sun heats up and we'll be okay.

Topped our stack; stooked till noon, relayed horses and worked binder till quitting time. Went to the dance at night, had a good time.

"Because of the vast distances in the universe, it is difficult for our instruments to see other star-systems as much more than tiny pinpoints of light."

Two boys on the top of Sulphur Mountain. Someone hears them talking about their climb and says, "Don't you guys know that water won't boil on a mountain? The air's too thin to boil! You were wasting your time even trying to make it boil!" Someone else chimes in with advice. "Take the trail when you go back down. We seen you two guys slippin' and slidin' down there in the shale. Someone pointed you out a couple of hours ago, and everybody's been havin' a laugh ever since. You two saps musta missed the sign! Nobody here climbed up the face! Everybody here took the easy walk up the trail!"

Meeting a country school teacher.
Making a couple of bridles.

Perhaps we peer beyond - other star systems - water won't boil - wasting your time - took the easy walk - what am I going to do - lasts a few seconds - no sense in closing my eyes - don't back into the belt - i'd like to be.

So, I'm twenty-three years old. Turned twenty-three in June. June twenty-second.

My dad died at fifty-three. That's thirty more years, if I die at fifty-three. Every day after that would be a bonus for me.

Sixty-three, seventy-three, eighty-three. Let's say I have sixty more years. What am I going to do with all that time?

The baker bakes the bread in the oven.
What he is and what he does is his gift.

Getting worried about my gloves. Hole in the left middle finger. Hope Tom remembered to bring extra gloves today. Pretty hard on this old finger if he forgot. Sun comes up of a sudden out here. Sunrise only lasts a few seconds. Not like at home. No sense closing my eyes at all. Every rut just jars them open. Soon be pulling into the field, sliding down and getting to work. Some day I'd like to just set on this wagon and never get off.

8:28 - 8:29 - 8:30 - 8:31- 8:32 - 8:33 - 8:34 - 8:35 - 8:36 - 8:37 - 8:38 - 8:39 - 8:40 - 8:41- 8:42 - 8:43 - 8:44 - 8:45 - 8:46 - 8:47 - 8:48 - 8:49 - 8:50 - 8:51 - 8:52 - 8:53 - 8:54 - 8:55 - 8:56 - 8:57 - 8:58 - 8:59 - 9:00 - 9:01 - 9:02 - 9:03 - 9:04 - 9:05 - 9:06 - 9:07 - 9:08 - 9:09.

A widow
planting
seeds.

A group of Hungarians dancing in a railroad yard.
A young boy delivering groceries with a pony and cart.
A greengrocer store near the docks.

Hoeing
the weeds
in summer.

Who are the people who won't let go?
Those who insist that you pay your dues?
Do they account for the deepest wrinkles in your brain?

Gathering in
the spoils
at harvest time.

Threshing, threshing, threshing. Up this morning before the sun. Threshing all day without a break. Pitching the sheaves up onto the thresher. Mind you don't back into the belt. The young boy brings a flagon of water to where we work. Least the water's nice and cold. You can feel it going down. Some day I'd like to be a water-boy.

Chapter 14

September is moving right along. Taking my pencil and making a little tick in the corner of the calendar. After supper every day. Unless I tumble into bed and catch up later. Walking miles every day. Covering a lot of ground. Miles and miles and miles. Wearing out a pair of gloves. Forgetting about the gloves and getting our hands full of thistles. Plenty of callouses on our hands and broken nails. Glad to have a rainy day. Train the colts, mend some harness, read a bit from the *World Book* and enjoy the meals.

Bright, crisp morning.

A rider firing a warning to a couple of rustlers.
A dreamer dreaming about the Great Divide.
Seeds which are stirring in the ground.

435 acres of grain.

A hunter taking a shot at a prairie chicken.
A woman cutting asparagus in a yard.
A herd of horses grazing in the grass.

A pleasant day today.

So what are your needs and what are your wishes?
What the steak and what the ice-cream?
What the water in the oasis you crawl towards?

9:10 - 9:11 - 9:12 - 9:13 - 9:14 - 9:15 - 9:16 - 9:17 - 9:18 - 9:19 - 9:20 - 9:21 - 9:22 - 9:23 - 9:24 - 9:25 - 9:26 - 9:27 - 9:28 - 9:29 - 9:30 - 9:31- 9:32 - 9:33 - 9:34 - 9:35 - 9:36 - 9:37 - 9:38 - 9:39 - 9:40 - 9:41- 9:42 - 9:43 - 9:44 - 9:45 - 9:46 - 9:47 - 9:48 - 9:49 - 9:50 - 9:51.

Dewdney talking as we wash up at the pump. Dewdney this and Dewdney that. Railway station, hardware store, small hotel. Everybody chuckling as he talks all through the meals. Undertaker if you ever need one. He's the local carpenter too. Make you some cupboards or a casket out of pine. On and on about such a great little town to live in as Dewdney BC. Eventually, he gets wise. Sees where the laughs are coming from. Sits quietly, chewing his food like everyone else. No more chuckles over Dewdney – the perfect town.

Sunshine and a heavy wind today. Generator windmill, 2' in diameter, roars like an aeroplane. Stooked all afternoon, wind burned our faces. Received a letter from Ken. Took picture of the colts and the Greyhound.

"When we measure the earth, we find that it is 21,600 geographical miles along the Equator, has 196,940,400 square miles of area and a volume of 259,980 million cubic miles."

Two Studebakers covered in chicken-shit in the shed. Siphonin' off the gasoline. Only half a bucket left. Enough for the rest of the afternoon. Tomorrow, I'll hitch the horses to the plough.

"Many people are living on their savings."

Making a little tick - tumble into bed - covering a lot of ground - plenty of callouses - train the colts - read a bit - enjoy the meals - a great little town - sunshine and heavy wind - 259,980 million cubic miles.

You know we almost went to Hong Kong. Or wherever those freighters go. The both of us lined up in the Vancouver yards.
Anywhere the ocean will take us. That's what both of us said one day. We'd been sleeping on a bench in Stanley Park.
Turned out every door was closed. Didn't have our seamen's card. 'Til then, I thought I was off to see the world.

*Who will pull the donkey cart
now the donkey's dead?*

Threshing, threshing, threshing. Feeling our way out to the barn. Nobody bothers to use a lantern. We know this place like braille. Just keep your hands in front of you. Point your way towards the barn and you'll be okay. Getting the harnesses off the pegs and buckling them on. Putting the feed bags on and feeling our way back to the house. Coffee and pancakes and all the trimmings. Tom's the first to head out to the barn again. By sunrise we'll be threshing out in the field.

Bright, crisp morning; run binder all day. We drive to the fields each morning, with eight horses ahead of a light wagon. We also drive a horse or team from the barn to the field it being a fifteen minute drive down the field.

"However, even cylindrical projections are only accurate at the Equator, with distortions increasing as one approaches the North and South poles."

Checking the days on the calendar.
Washing up at the pump.

Madame Florina closes the door. The sun casts the young man's shadow on the frosted glass. She puts her glasses on and fumbles with the lock. She has a stricken look on her face.

Covered in chicken-shit - half a bucket left - sleeping on a bench - every door was closed - off to see the world - feeling our way - are accurately shown - distortions are increased - the young man's shadow - a stricken look.

I keep going to see these gypsies. Never believe a word they say. But for some reason, I'm drawn to them all the same.
There was one of them at Port Stanley. That's a beach not far from home. And another one at the Calgary Stampede.
I don't believe in the supernatural. But I've heard things I can't explain. Two of them now have told me the very same thing.

The vase was glued and put on the mantel
and the hole was turned to the back.
A gaping hole that only the family could see.

Attending church with Miss Trevelean. A lot of old hymns that I know from home. 'I shall cling to the old rugged cross.' Guess everyone sings the same ones everywhere. Looks quite nice in her Sunday getup. Nice touch with the wild-flowers pinned to her blouse. Telling her I have a suit at home. No sense bringing it here on the hobo. Surprised that Charlie had his mom send out his suit. Telling her why I didn't borrow it. ''Til my burden at last I lay down.' Her voice is nice to listen to. I haven't sung these hymns since I was a boy.

Two railroad workers walking past the police.
The crust of the outer surface of the earth.
The birth of a baby in a small town.

Monday September 12 1932 - Tuesday September 13 1932 - Wednesday September 14 1932 - Thursday September 15 1932 - Friday September 16 1932 - Saturday September 17 1932.

Air, water, food?
Some colts to raise; some wood to shape?
Sturdy roof, warm stove, a book to read?

"And all the kids grew up and went to school and got jobs and got married and started having families of their own."

Marquette - Rosser - Woodman - Winnipeg - East Selkirk - Molson - Whitemouth - Rennie - Ingolf - Kenora - Scovil - Pine - Vermillion Bay - Eagle River - Dryden - Raleigh - Ignace - Bonheur - Niblock - Upsala - Raith.

A mortgage paper torn in half on a kitchen table.
Men in suits and ties gathered around a fire.
Cattle grazing in a field as dry as dust.

Threshing, threshing, threshing. Only two miles from the house. Nice to think we'll be coming home at noon, putting the feed bag on and then out to the field again. Forking the sheaves in the threshing machine. Yesterday we threshed all day. Out in the dark and back in the dark. Finished our supper at nine p.m. The moon shone through the window as I tumbled into bed.

Stooked till noon; finished cutting and stooking 435 acres of grain today. Colts performed like old horses today. We drove them 2 miles this afternoon. Housed the binder till next fall.

"New knowledge and past experience merge to make a forecast of the expected weather for the foreseeable future."

"There are one hundred thousand transients in the four Western provinces."

A boy sits on a chair at the end of the table. Nibbling a biscuit and sipping a cup of tea. The faces are ruddy and tanned and smiling. They sing the songs of over 'ome. His father plays the concertina. The music and the singing fill the room.

Things I can't explain - a gaping hole - families of their own - out in the dark - back in the dark - tumbled into bed - his new knowledge - the record of the past - to make his forecast - the music and the singing.

Don't know what to make of these *World Books*. Some family moved out and left them all behind. I read them in the barn whenever it rains.

There's a few of them in every house. The Culham family has two. Mr.

Culham doesn't think they're what they're cracked up to be.

Nothing in there about making a harness. Or planting wheat or planing wood. The Introduction says it's all the best thoughts in the world.

Where to land?
Where to nest?
Where to be?

Threshing, threshing, threshing. Harnessing the team by the light of the moon. Getting the feed to all the horses. Hearing the whistle at 4:28 as the train goes by. Threshing 'til three o'clock. Hard to pitch the sheaves in the wagon. A strong wind blowing it all right back again. Taking the sheaves right off the fork. Wind and rain delay for two hours. Pulling my cap down over my forehead and closing my eyes.

A pleasant day today. Amused ourselves reading etc. Attended church in the evening.

"Heavenly bodies which give off light which is generated by their own resources have been called 'stars.'"

He harnesses up the colts and hitches up the cart. He tosses a couple of arm-loads of firewood in just to give them the sense of a load. A couple more training sessions and maybe he'll take them into town. Get a haircut and maybe bring back a small load of coal. They'll soon be earning their keep. Give the Culhams a lot of service in the years to come.

Threshing in the fields.
Working against the wind.

Cracked up to be - all the best thoughts - wind and rain delay - can be defined - shines by its own light - at its peak and its prime - yours the key - catch the wind just right - scattered all over the field - gives us their monikers.

I really feel terrible about what happened to Len Yarwood. Charlie feels awful too. When we got that letter, we didn't know what to do.

Len had that wheat field at its peak and its prime. And the next thing you know, the hail just came along and wiped him out. Took everything he'd built up over the year.

I'm not the kind of person to cry, but if you wanted to cry your eyes out, that would be the time – reading that letter from Len addressed to Charlie and me. He was going to write to England to tell them the news.

Whoever they are they speak as if they know.

Every night a different voice with similar words.
"Yours the key that locks you in or lets you out."

Threshing, threshing, threshing. Working from the windward side of the wagon. Hefting the fork up in the air and dumping the sheaves down into the basket. If you catch the wind just right it can help you throw. If you don't it will dump it all right down on your head. Throw too high and you can throw it right over the rack and it's gone for good. Scattered all over the field or the other guys. Charlie says he hates the wind. I liked it, myself, 'til I tried to load a wagon. No such wind like this back home on Ontario farms.

9:10 - 9:11 - 9:12 - 9:13 - 9:14 - 9:15 - 9:16 - 9:17 - 9:18 - 9:19 - 9:20 - 9:21 - 9:22 - 9:23 - 9:24 - 9:25 - 9:26 - 9:27 - 9:28 - 9:29 - 9:30 - 9:31- 9:32 - 9:33 - 9:34 - 9:35 - 9:36 - 9:37 - 9:38 - 9:39 - 9:40 - 9:41- 9:42 - 9:43 - 9:44 - 9:45 - 9:46 - 9:47 - 9:48 - 9:49 - 9:50 - 9:51.

A rabbit nibbles
quickly
at the lettuce.

A gurgling creek about two feet wide.
A binder with its canvas belts jammed.
A group of hoboes sleeping on a tender of coal.

His ears are
as large as
nature knows how to make.

Are people a luxury or a necessity?
A burning obsession or an idle thought?
Perhaps a confection to a person who doesn't like sweets?

Does he hear
the dog's nose
as it sniffs the air?

Lining up at the pump at the end of the working day. Boots thumping on the porch as the triangle rings. Turns out that Dewdney knows Hungarian. Knows a word for every food. Points them out as he gives us their monikers. On this table, we have ásványvíz, hizlal, burgonya, besóz and megvajaz. Well, what do you know about that? Everything that's on the table has a Hungarian name! Everybody at the table trying to pronounce the words as we eat. Pass the ásványvíz, Charlie says, and everyone laughs. We'd starve in Dewdney if we had to order food!

Chapter 15

Too wet to work today out in the fields. Charlie whittling himself a whistle while I read. I miss everything at home, Charlie is saying. Miss the woods. Miss the green fields. Miss the running water in the streams. Miss the fruit trees and all the variety in the gardens. I miss going to the pond to swim or heading down to the beach. Everything out here's the same every day. Back home there's change all the time. I'd be glad to come back any time to visit, or to work if I don't have a job, but I wouldn't want to live out here at all.

Tired and blistered at night.

A boy growing a moustache to look older.
A hand filled with thousands of stinging nettles.
Ancestral voices calling from ancient times.

Singsong around the piano.

A palm with two pennies, a nickel and a dime.
A group of men cooking soup in a pot.
Grasshoppers blotting out the sky.

A feeling of snow.

Suppose your father had lived a lot longer?
Or if your mother had died quite young?
Or if one of your brothers or sisters hadn't been born?

9:52 - 9:53 - 9:54 - 9:55 - 9:56 - 9:57 - 9:58 - 9:59 - 10:00 - 10:01 - 10:02 - 10:03 - 10:04 - 10:05 - 10:06 - 10:07 - 10:08 - 10:09 - 10:10 - 10:11 10:12 - 10:13 - 10:14 - 10:15 - 10:16 - 10:17 - 10:18 - 10:19 - 10:20 - 10:21 - 10:22 - 10:23 - 10:24 - 10:25 - 10:26 - 10:27 - 10:28 - 10:29 - 10:30 - 10:31- 10:32 - 10:33 - 10:34.

Inviting the school teacher over for the weekend. The two of us and Charlie taking the greyhound and going after rabbits. No rabbits, but we have a good gallop anyway. Too wet to work but too nice to stay inside. Pitching a few loads on when things dry out a bit. Miss Trevelean and Mrs. Culham driving the team. All of us going to the dance in town at night. Charlie warning me that the summer will end and I'll have to go back home. Me telling Charlie I'm thinking the same and that the school marm's probably thinking the same thing too.

Drove three miles to start threshing today. Cleaned off 88 acres and finished tired and blistered at night. We use six teams in the field and two hauling grain.

"Calculations show that the Arctic and Antarctic regions of the earth account for 8.4 percent of its area, with 51.4 percent within the two temperate regions and 40 percent within the Tropic regions."

He taps the pencil on the paper. His wife pulls back her chair and sets another cup of tea on the table and sits down beside him. He tosses the pencil towards her. He leans back in his chair. She frowns and puts her glasses on and takes her turn with the numbers on the list.

"Though incomes are in decline, the burden of debt for families and businesses remains the same."

Too wet to work - a feeling of snow - tired and blistered - earth's total area - 51.4 percent - fellow fixing the tracks - gangrene sets in - nothin' you can do - pile of old bones - hanging on for dear old life.

There was this fellow fixing the tracks. And he lost his footing and fell against the train. And he smashed his mouth and rolled on down the slope.
And Charlie and me went down to help him. The foreman called down to us that it was only a Chinese. We helped him onto the train and stopped the bleeding.
We took him to a station and helped him down. We did what we could, but you can only do so much. He was all alone and a long, long way from home.

Chances are
your life will be more
than a sequence of chances.

Lots of things to do on a Sunday. Morning gallop with Miss Trevelean. Tom deciding to shoot the horse with the broken leg. Tried to save it with a sling and some ointment but the leg set in to rot. Once gangrene sets in, you know, why there's nothin' you can do. This was a darn good horse but I ain't gonna let 'im suffer. You and Charlie can drag 'im out, if you want, to the slough. Charlie and me dragging the dead carcass a mile out onto the prairie. Unhitching him and leaving him there alongside the pile of old bones. Hollering and galloping all the way back to the barnyard. These big old horses loving the chance to stretch their legs. Me and Charlie hanging on for dear old life.

It rained during the nite. Today I brought the school teacher over for the weekend. In the evening we had a singsong around the piano.

"Over the years, cartographers have shown a preference for cylindrical projections over any other method of projection."

Thinking about Ontario.
Dragging a horse with a broken leg.

I could be sitting here forever. Don't dare to go back home. Don't dare to go ahead. I ain't gonna move from here until I can play this tune.

Fellow fixing the tracks - lost his footing - did what we could - cylindrical projections - sitting here forever - until I can play - a gleaming scythe - truth cannot be added to - like water or like wine - rack completely over.

My father was fifty-three years old when he died. My mother was forty-three years old when my father died. My sister, Margaret, was eighteen years old when my father died.

My sister, Hilda, was sixteen years old when my father died. My brother, Bob, was fourteen years old when my father died. My brother, Ken, was six years old when my father died.

Ever wonder what death will look like when it comes to claim you? In the movies it's Father Time with a gleaming scythe. In real life, it could be a boxcar and a hook and a chain.

> *"There is no gain without a loss.*
> *No advance that is not a retreat."*
> *The sap ran slowly; the scarred bark throbbed.*
> *It seemed to be the leaves that made the sound.*
> *"Truth cannot be added to, like water or like wine.*
> *Wisdom gained must be paid with wisdom lost."*

Getting the sense that she's coming to an end. A dark morning and threatening rain. Stronger winds than we've ever had before. Making it so hard to work that we quit at three o'clock. A man and a rack completely over. The loads are like sails as they catch the wind. Nobody hurt but Mr. Culham says it's too windy to work. Everyone says that it won't be long before there's snow.

Woven rings for sale on a railroad platform.
A woman on a verandah reading a letter.
Two boys cutting grass in a prairie slough.

Sunday September 18 1932 - Monday September 19 1932 - Tuesday September 20 1932 - Wednesday September 21 1932 - Thursday September 22 1932 - Friday September 23 1932 - Saturday September 24 1932.

What if your twin sister had lived?
Or if you had died instead of her?
Would your brothers and your sisters be the same?

"And the man and woman lived on and he retired from the railroad and they went on trips to all kinds of places around the world."

Buda - Kaminisigula - Ft. William - Port Arthur - Loon - Pearl - Nipigon - Dublin - Rossport - Schreiber - Jack Fish Bay - Middleton - Heron Bay - Struthers - Brenner - White River - Amyot - Grasset - Missanabie - Dalton.

A jackrabbit running across a field.
A team of horses breaking clods with a disc.
The waters of a crystal-clear mountain lake.

Up at four a.m. and feeding the horses. Threshing for twelve hours straight. Clearing a hundred acres of wheat for twelve-hundred bushel. Surprised to learn that there's such a low yield. Forty bushel to the acre on farms back home in Ontario. Here they're lucky if an acre clears fifteen. The Culhams have twelve hundred acres. If all they had was a hundred acres, they'd starve to death.

Quite dark this morning and looking like rain. Wind attained a high velocity today, and as the wind blew our loads off, we quit at 3 pm. One man and rack was blown completely over, no damage. There's been a feeling of snow in the air all day.

"As soon as the forecast of expected weather-trends is ready, it is passed on, via news agencies, to the public."

"The minimum wage is twenty-five cents an hour."

He bounces along on his father's shoulders. What's for supper? How long you been waiting? The lunch-pail swings at his father's side. Did you get wet when it started to rain? That nasty rabbit ever come back? The two of them stride across the grass. Where is your mom? Where are the kids? Are the berries ready to pick? What was the nicest thing that happened to you today?

Too windy to work - man and woman lived on - retired from the railroad - surprised to learn - moulded into one forecast - wake up in a sweat - dream is always the same - walls are moving in - seem to wake up - always be looking.

You know, sometimes I wake up in a sweat. Takes me a while to catch my breath. And then I realize I've been dreaming and then it's okay.

And the dream is always the same. I'm lying on my back on a slab of stone. It's so dark that I don't know where I am.

And there's a weight that's crushing my chest. And the walls are moving in. And that's about the time I seem to wake up.

If he doesn't find his little red ball, thought the gnome,
he will have sunlight and he will have rain,
he will have laughter and he will have pain,
but he will always be looking in the garden for the little red ball.

Feeling lonely at the dance. Saturday night and nothing to do. Lady's Aid Social at the hall in town. Borrowed a lighter pair of shoes. Leaning against the wall and feeling stiff and tired and sore. Cleared a hundred acres again today. Fixed the pump and caught a pig. Feeling depressed as I stand here watching everyone dancing. The threshing is coming along on schedule. Soon be time to head back home. Won't miss the work, but I'm going to miss the West. Missing the teacher, I guess, so I'm feeling a little sad.

Got up at 4 am this morning, drove over in the car to feed the horses. We threshed hard all day today twelve hours straight. Cleared 100 acres of wheat which yielded 1200 bushel.

"It would appear that most stars in the heavens do not change position relative to other stars in their vicinities."

He trudges along the highway. The day is hot, the air is humid and his feet are sore. The *World Book* sits at the bottom of his pack. *"To the people who live upon it, the earth is the most important part of the universe, and it is difficult to think of it as being a very small unit in a universe the size of which is beyond conception."* Tempted to leave it on a fencepost along the road. Or stuff it into a mailbox if it would fit. Like a catalogue from Eatons for someone to find. A lot of extra weight to carry when you're hot and tired and hungry.

"*The world at your command on the wings of words.*" Feels a lot more like a brick than a set of wings.

> Threshing wheat for twelve hours.
> Talking on the porch.

> *Stiff and tired and sore - time to head back home - threshed hard all day - stars remained fixed - leave it on a fencepost - hot and tired and hungry - more like a brick - world at your command - things didn't work out - only talks to me.*

I had a good talk with Mr. Culham. It was raining and we were sitting on the porch. The rain poured off the roof as we sat and talked.

He was talking about the early days. When he and his wife came out to the West. They came out here, he said, because things didn't work out for them in the East.

"I'll tell you, Cyr", he said, "there are times you think you can move somewhere else and leave all your troubles behind. But the truth of the matter is, that no matter where you are, life has a way of comin' along and findin' you. Life seems to know exactly where you are."

> *The puppet lay back down on the shelf.*
> *He shrugged his shoulders into the strings.*
> *As the sun rose, the puppeteer opened his eyes.*

A lovely, calm September morning. Today's the day Dewdney goes home. I'll miss him always talking about his home town. He only talks to me now, since the other fellows all laugh. Out for supper at the Cartwrights' and caught in the rain. Everything here just looks so desolate when it's wet. The horses' hooves suck up the mud as we plod along. Nothing but puddles everywhere and the absence of trees. A depressing look to everything I see.

> *9:52 - 9:53 - 9:54 - 9:55 - 9:56 - 9:57 - 9:58 - 9:59 - 10:00 - 10:01 - 10:02 - 10:03 - 10:04 - 10:05 - 10:06 - 10:07 - 10:08 - 10:09 - 10:10 - 10:11 10:12 - 10:13 - 10:14 - 10:15 - 10:16 - 10:17 - 10:18 - 10:19 - 10:20 - 10:21 - 10:22 - 10:23 - 10:24 - 10:25 - 10:26 - 10:27 - 10:28 - 10:29 - 10:30 - 10:31- 10:32 - 10:33 - 10:34.*

> *A young man*
> *whistling*
> *for his brother.*

> *A man tumbling off a boxcar in the mountains.*
> *A thousand people dancing on a street.*

A man who has retired from the railroad.

*A young man
showing off
a cart and horse.*

Do we live inside other people?
Do other people live inside us?
Or do all of us walk along on separate paths?

*Fresh vegetables
delivered
daily to your house.*

Setting the straw-stacks on fire. To mark the end of the harvest. At last, the threshing is done. Ride like the wind on horseback! Hold the torch at the end of your arm! Be careful not to singe your horse as you swing your arm! Ride from haystack to haystack! Go like the devil and set 'em on fire! Acres and acres of blazing straw. Blazing stacks of fire as far as the eye can see. Burning brightly against the night sky. Dotted all across the fields – a ribbon of fire.

Chapter 16

One of those end-of-September days. Spending the morning drawing grain. Wheat and oats and barley. From the fields to the granaries and back again. Four miles there and four miles back. A wagon-master like we used to see in the movies. Pair of gloves. Holding the reins. Buggy-whip stirring up the flies. Settling down inside a rut and up again. Not so hot as back in August in Alberta. Beautiful weather when it isn't pouring rain.

A lovely, calm September morning.

Twenty neighbours having a good old prairie feast.
Two riders under the dome of the Northern Lights.
An old man giving a diary to a boy.

Beautiful day today, like Indian summer.

Thunder and lightning flashing in a canyon.
A hay wagon creaking slowly along a trail.
A customer squeezing a tomato.

A fitting end to our departure.

Does time flow through us or around us?
Is time the poison in our blood?
Is time a stream in which we can drown or we can drink?

10:35 - 10:36 - 10:37 - 10:38 - 10:39 - 10:40 - 10:41- 10:42 - 10:43 - 10:44 - 10:45 - 10:46 - 10:47 - 10:48 - 10:49 - 10:50 - 10:51- 10:52 - 10:53 - 10:54 - 10:55 - 10:56 - 10:57 - 10:58 - 10:59 - 11:00 - 11:01 - 11:02 - 11:03 - 11:04 - 11:05 - 11:06 - 11:07 - 11:08 - 11:09 - 11:10 - 11:11 - 11:12 - 11:13 - 11:14 - 11:15 - 11:16.

Tanking wheat and barley. To the siding and back again. Charlie and me both have our own outfit. Making a little wagon train. Going out shooting game with Ivan. Hungarian partridge and prairie chicken. Dusting the fir off some jackrabbits but they all get away.

A lovely, calm September morning. "Dewdney" went home today. Went out for supper, got caught in the rain. Some localitys here are very desolate looking, nature of the ground and absence of trees, give the land a depressed look.

"Assuming that there are 250,000 square miles of undiscovered land under the Arctic, and 2,500,000 square miles under the Antarctic, the entire land mass of earth can be estimated to be 54,807, 420 square miles in area."

An apple orchard! All my own! Abundance is the word that I would use! Harvest time is the payoff time! All that time waiting for things to grow! All that watering and pruning and trimming! Now the bows droop down with their bounty! The trees are in rows like knights in service to their lord! A good long ladder for reaching the top! Plenty of baskets to fill up and store! Lots of time to dig me a fruit-cellar, cool and spacious! Let the winter come on with its storms! Doesn't matter what cold or what snow! I've got apples here for winter and into the spring! Abundance, abundance, abundance! Abundance has to be the final word!

"There are people who are working for only eight dollars a month."

A wagon-master - inside a rut - a fitting end - on the assumption - remain to be discovered - the supposed antarctic continent - watering and pruning and trimming - lots of time - what cold or what snow - abundance, abundance, abundance.

You know, my mother plants a garden. Cans a lot of food in the autumn. She's got jars of preserves just bulging on the shelves.
But it drives my mother crazy. Rabbits tunnel in under the fence. Every summer they get in and have a feast.
So we got ourselves a dog. But the dog can't seem to catch them. Every once in a while I find a new hole in the fence.

The flowers will bloom in a rage of colour.
More than I can ever hope to conceive.

Raining again in the morning. Shooting pigeons in the barn. Adding to our wildfowl catch of yesterday. Twenty minutes of heavy hail. No major damage to the crops, Mr. Culham says. Not like the storms we have back East. Up and gone in twenty minutes from a clear blue sky.

Beautiful day today, like Indian summer. Picked up potatoes, that we ploughed up with a gang plough.

"A map is always an uneasy compromise in terms of accuracy between the three elements of direction, scale and position."

Driving a team and wagon.
Watching a hail storm from the porch.

Strong winds in the orchard! Blowing right across my property and onto the neighbour's land! Taking the ladder down before I take a tumble! The trees are bending in the wind! Dipping their branches right down to the ground! Apples bouncing like hailstones everywhere around! The wind is getting stronger! Tumbling the baskets over and spilling! Apples rolling along on the ground! Picking up speed and attacking my orchard! Ripping apples right off the trees and blasting them right across the fence to the neighbour's place! Apples whizzing past my head! When is the wind going to die down? Can the blast get any stronger? Everything I've worked so hard for! Torn from the trees and blasting away! Putting a basket on my head and ducking and dodging! Is the wind picking up or dying down!

Rabbits tunnel in - hope to conceive - no major damage - a graphical representation - the three basic requirements - bending in the wind - picking up speed - attacking my orchard - worked so hard for - had an accident one time.

I had an accident one time. Put the brake-stick in the wheel and it snapped in two. Could have been worse if I'd been caught by the wheels of the train.
Put my hand on some nettles one time. Admiring the scenery in the desert. Put my hand on a cactus and had a sore hand for a week.
Still, I've had a lot of good times. One day you're crouching in a box-car with bullets whizzing by. Then a ride in a car full of flowers on the way to a fair.

The traffic will change with the choices and the seasons.
Know that the house that you are building will outlast you.

Polishing the car after dinner. Mrs. Culham and me making her shine like new. Driving over to the school to see the teacher. Quite a sight to see all these kids. Pouring like water out the door as the school-bell rings. Down the steps and onto their horses and up on their wagons. All racing as fast as they can to get back home. A very nice visit – just the two of us. Cleaning off the blackboards and emptying the trash. Cleaning the ashes out of the stove and splitting some firewood. A moonlit evening by the time I'm driving back.

An article on the rotation of the earth.
Two boys huddling inside a piece of machinery.
A stew that does not boil on the side of a mountain.

Sunday September 25 1932 - Monday September 26 1932 - Tuesday September 27 1932 - Wednesday September 28 1932 - Thursday September 29 1932 - Friday September 30 1932.

Does each of us light a candle the day we are born?
Do we hold that candle cupped as we bend in the wind?
Do we share our candle's glow as we make our way?

"And the man died – of course – though we can't say whether his retirement was long or was short."

Chapleau - Kinogama - Woman River - Ramsay - Bistcotasing - Metagama - Pogamising - Cartier - Sudbury - Romford - Wanup - Worthington - Wanikewan - Point au Baril - Shawabaga - MacTier - Bala - Medonte - Essa - Beston.

Crops flat as a carpet and covered in hail.
A tractor ploughing a field in a cloud of dust.
Work-camp inmates idling on a porch.

Helping Mr. Culham disc. Taking the team for a couple of rounds. A twenty-foot swath. Eight horses. Seven acres to a round. He walks along beside me, giving me tips for handling the horses. Says I'm catchin' on like a pro. Charlie and me are both in top form, but my back and arms aren't used to working a team. Everyone works quite hard out here. Different kind of work from the railroad, that's for sure.

Drew a load of grain to town. Washed some clothes, and made some preparations for our departure to the east. Done some discing with the eight horse outfit, Charlie and I drove a heard of cattle over to the old place for fall grazing. I don't envy a cowboy now!

"Despite our reliance on weather-forecasts, for business and for pleasure, no meteorologist is able to say that a weather prediction, no matter how scientific, comes with a guarantee."

"Radical Canadians are forming new political parties."

Lashing myself to an apple tree! The wind is howling through the orchard! Some of these trees are cracking their limbs! Feels as if some of them are going to come right out by the roots! Seems to be calm on the neighbour's land! Every apple seems to be landing on his side! Tightening the ropes as best I can! I'll stay here 'til the last tree is uprooted! 'Til the last apple is lying on the ground! Will there be any apples left? Bruised and battered on the trees or windfalls lying in the grass? Apples whizzing by my head! The wind is tearing at my clothes! Surely the wind is getting stronger! These trees are straining at their roots! Liable to rip up any time! This was my stake for the coming winter! This orchard is all I have! What in the world am I going to do now?

Could have been worse - hand on some nettles - bullets whizzing by - a car full of flowers - the choices and the seasons - a very nice visit - we can't say - giving me tips - made some preparations - makes no claims.

Did I tell you I was keeping a diary? There was an old hobo who talked like a professor. He gave me a diary and that's when I started to write.

Don't worry about what to write, he said. Just note the places and times. Just do that and you'll start to see what it's all about.

So, anyway, I just keep jotting things down. Dates and places – not much more. Just a matter of keeping track of what we've done.

Wisdom grows a little flower
on a sunny day.

Ivan winning his little battle. Been going on for over a month. Started to talk about it when Charlie and me first arrived. Asked us to back him about the safety of the travel and all. His parents mulled it as he talked. His mom held out a long ways past where his dad gave in. A chance to see his relatives and look around Ontario. He was born here and he's never been to the East. So he's going to come back home with us. The glamour of riding the rails. Stay in St. Thomas with me and Charlie while we take him to see Toronto and Niagara Falls.

Our last Sunday in Sask. Slept all morning, and went for a keen gallop after breakfast. Had two accomplished girls, piano player and singer, down for the afternoon. Had the teacher down, to put a fitting end to our departure. We sure beat out the ragtime.

"However, there are some stars which do seem to change their positions, as can be observed by watching them, via telescope, on successive nights."

She hears the mailman's clatter as he rattles the letterbox. She opens the door and takes the letter out. Cold in October, so she quickly closes the door. Hi Mom. Looks like the harvest is coming to an end. We'll be starting for home pretty soon. The crops are almost off and there's snow in the air. The Culhams have been really good to Charlie and me. Ivan Culham wants to come back East and visit some of his relatives, so I said we'd put him up for as long as he wants. He says just a few days and then he'll be moving along. I figure I'll clear about two hundred dollars by the time we're all done here. Not bad for a summer's work. How'd the apples do this year? Did you get to keep some lettuce? Did the dog keep the rabbits at bay? Sorry I didn't get everything done before I left. I figure I'll build that new fence I promised just as soon as I get back home. Say hello to Ken and Hilda and the dog. And Bob and Margaret over in Detroit whenever you can.

    Visiting with the teacher.
    Controlling an eight-horse disc.

The complete accuracy - bruised and battered - straining at their roots - what in the world - keeping a diary - winning his little battle - snow in the air - the end of the trail - dints in the cedar shingles - have a good life.

What was that old guy trying to tell me? That old hobo in the Toronto yards. Picked me out and said I was different from all the rest.
He gave me a brand-new diary. With a date on every page. Told me he didn't need it 'cause he'd reached the end of the trail.
Told me don't write what you think or feel. Just write down what people do and what they say. Some days I just write 'stooking' and fall into bed.

*   We do not live by bread alone.*
*   So what will you and what will your gift be?*

A letter from back in Alberta. Addressed to Charlie and me. Hey, it's from Len Yarwood! What does he say? Looks like he's been wiped out by the hail! Says it ruined all his crop! Had a bumper crop and now it's all destroyed! Says the hailstones put big dints in the cedar shingles of the roof! We sure don't ever have hail like that back in the East. Says he's thinking of giving his land to his brother and going on back to St. Thomas. Says the fields look like a carpet, the hail was so bad. Says he's wondering if the Anderson farm would be willing to take him back. Charlie and me trying to think of something to write back to Len. His first year out here and the hail has wiped him out. Len was sitting on a bumper crop. Hard to think of him walking over those ruined fields.

*   10:35 - 10:36 - 10:37 - 10:38 - 10:39 - 10:40 - 10:41- 10:42 - 10:43 - 10:44 - 10:45 - 10:46 - 10:47 - 10:48 - 10:49 - 10:50 - 10:51- 10:52 - 10:53*

- 10:54 - 10:55 - 10:56 - 10:57 - 10:58 - 10:59 - 11:00 - 11:01 - 11:02 - 11:03 - 11:04 - 11:05 - 11:06 - 11:07 - 11:08 - 11:09 - 11:10 - 11:11 - 11:12 - 11:13 - 11:14 - 11:15 - 11:16.

*A young man
hugging
his mom.*

*A drink of water which vanishes in the hand.
A train with no visible means of locomotion.
Straw stacks on fire on a prairie field.*

*Shaking hands
with his
younger brother.*

Do shadows gather as the darkness closes in?
Do they reach their candles out to the dying flame?
Do we light their wicks before we pass away?

*He turns
and slings his pack
onto his back.*

Our last Sunday in Saskatchewan. Sleeping all morning and a gallop after breakfast. Music in the parlour in the afternoon. Visiting piano player and singer from beyond the next town. Singing everything from hymns to ragtime tunes. Big feast and lots of talking. Last meeting with Miss Trevelean. Nice of her to come along and see us off. She'll stay here in Saskatchewan. I'll return to Ontario. She'll teach school, get married, have children – grow old and have a good life. Says she'll forget about this summer. Says I will too.

Chapter 17

A perfect October morning. A heavy frost on the ground. Atmosphere exceptionally clear. Discing with the eight-horse team all morning and afternoon. Packing the saddle and the suitcase for shipping to the East. Two hundred dollars tied up in my bundle. A ride to the Station at nine p.m. Saying goodbye and thanks to the Culhams – Ainsley and Mae. Waiting for the midnight train. Choosing the hopper of a combine. Charlie and me both clambering in. Ivan squeezing in alongside us. The metal is cold as the devil. Like being in the tower of a submarine.

In company with 19 others.

A dream in which the walls are closing in.
The unknown size of the universe.
A huge roll of tickets to a country fair.

Riding on the hurricane deck.

A Model-T Ford up on blocks.
A banker and a farmer arguing on a sidewalk.
A little girl shivering in a shack.

Extracted a quart of milk.

Are you a child of Oak Street?
A child of St. Thomas?
A child of Ontario?

11:17 - 11:18 - 11:19 - 11:20 - 11:21 - 11:22 - 11:23 - 11:24 - 11:25 - 11:26 - 11:27 - 11:28 - 11:29 - 11:30 - 11:31- 11:32 - 11:33 - 11:34 - 11:35 - 11:36 - 11:37 - 11:38 - 11:39 - 11:40 - 11:41- 11:42 - 11:43 - 11:44 - 11:45 - 11:46 - 11:47 - 11:48 - 11:49 - 11:50 - 11:51- 11:52 - 11:53 - 11:54 - 11:55 - 11:56 - 11:57 - 11:58 - 11:59.

A very, very cold night. Riding in this hopper is sure a mistake. Jumping off at every stop and running to keep warm. God help the poor devils who have to live life on the trains. Taking my boots off in a gale and rubbing my feet to try to restore my circulation. Ivan is proving a cheerful traveller. Making jokes with his frosty breath. Be nice to show him around Ontario. Take him dancing at the Royal York. Bob and Margaret over in Detroit. Nabisco factory and Niagara Falls. There'll be plenty of things to do when we get back home.

Arrived in Winnipeg at 3 am. Left on a wheat drag, ridding the tender at 6 am. Girl in boys clothes rode this train. Saw deer, partridge and porcupine. Had dinner in Kenora Ont. Arrived in Ignace, Lake of the Woods country, at midnite. Had supper in the sandhouse. Rode the tender again in company with 19 others and arrived in Ft. William rather cold.

"It has been estimated that if the earth's surface was level, the entire globe would be completely under water."

She lies there on the coal. Impossible to sleep with all these thoughts going through her head. All of these bodies lying around her. All of them men. Hope this get-up works okay. Smeared some coal-dust on my face just as soon as I could. Hope they welcome me when I get there. Couldn't think of anywhere else to go. Coffee shop wasn't making any money, so I can't blame them for letting me go. Offered to work for just my food, but they still said no. Once in a while a poke in the ribs when one of them rolls over. Gotta sleep with one eye open all the time. Really scary when some of them stare. These two young guys seem okay, but you never know. They told me to just keep on the way I'm going. No idea what I'm gonna find at the end of the road. Least I got a possibility. For now I got it at least. That's more than most of these guys here got. If they don't take me in, I don't know where I'll go.

"It is the young of the country who are paying the heaviest price."

A heavy frost - on the hurricane deck - help the poor devils - a cheerful traveller - girl in boys clothing - the solid crust of the earth - impossible to sleep - anywhere else to go - one eye open - what I'm gonna find.

I like working with those colts. Like to see them frisking in the fields. My grandfather worked with horses, my mother said.
    I've been working with horses at home. Charlie works with horses as well. Took a horse, once, through the jumps at the Winter Fair.
    When it's raining I go to the barn and work on some harnesses for the colts. I'm really pleased with the way they're coming along. I'm training them to pull the little cart.

*Life is short
said the old man
to the boy.*

Gathering round a jungle fire. Every kind of person on the bum. Pretty cheerful for down and out. Regaled by an old and very wise hobo. Telling a story for every town from here to the coast. The fire and the stew are taking the sting off the bitter cold. Jumping a wheat train at midnight. Arriving at Brandon at eight a.m. Can't believe the bite of the cold. Using our heads and changing our clothes. Putting our overalls on and talking to a conductor and getting a ride in the caboose of a stock train as far as Winnipeg.

Cop tried to run us in at MacTier. Jumped on in spite of him and high-balled thru to Tottenham, where we stayed the night with Ivan's relatives. I got my first Ontario apple in the neck while riding on the hurricane deck of a freight. We figured there would be an R.C.M.P cordon at Toronto.

"In addition, a good map should contain a legend which alerts the map-reader as to the difference between True North and Magnetic North."

Packing a suitcase for shipping home.
Freezing on a northern train.

He lies on the coal with his eyes wide open. Now and again he wipes some coal-dust from his eye. Never been as far East as Ontario. Be nice to see Toronto before I go back. Got my relatives' addresses in my bindle. Dad says they'll all take me in and show me around. Mom sent some letters on ahead, so they know I'm comin'. Nice of Cyril and Charlie to teach me the ropes. Wouldn't want to be travellin' alone. They're gonna show me around for a while. I'll stay with them for a couple of days. Cyril mentioned some places to go. Detroit, Buffalo, Niagara Falls. These two really get around. Must be nice to just take off and ride the rails. Saskatchewan is nice and all – Saskatchewan is home – but it'll be exciting to get to see a bit of the world.

More than most - I don't know where - frisking in the fields - through the jumps - life is short - the bite of the cold - apple in the neck - does not correspond - deviation between the two - to be travellin' alone.

You know, we stopped at the Great Divide. Got off the train and read the sign and looked around. Sat on a rock and had some sandwiches and a drink.

Looked like any other place with rock and water. Just a little creek about two feet wide and not very deep. Without the sign you wouldn't know where you are.

But that's where the waters were parting. Flowing East and flowing West. Every drop that fell on those rocks had somewhere to go.

Burst the grapes
one by one
in your mouth.

Spending a wonderful day in Port Arthur. Washing up at the Y and spending ten cents on a meal. A great big warehouse with tables of food. Soup on electric burners. Urns of coffee – help yourself. Cold meats on platters – left over from the restaurants. Stale cakes and day-old cookies for dessert. Whole families in line, with each child holding a dime. Everybody in the family eating their fill. Waiting to catch an East-bound train. Lounging around the waterfront. A deep blue haze hanging over the water. Grain boats coming and going all day. Makes me wish I had my easel and my paints. The most lazy and enjoyable day of the whole darn trip.

A hand tossing pennies on a table.
A tree that speaks of wisdom lost and gained.
A letter with news for the people back home.

Saturday October 1 1932 - Sunday October 2 1932 - Monday October 3 1932 - Tuesday October 4 1932.

A child of Canada?
A child of England?
A child of Europe?

"And late one October, in the middle of the night, the man died, in bed, with his wife beside him, in the house that he had built with his own two hands."

Bolton - Tottenham - Toronto - Mississauga - Milton - Oakville - Bronte - Waterdown - St. George - Paris - Princeton - Woodstock - Ingersoll - Salford - Mt. Elgin - Tillsonburg - Corinth - Richmond - Aylmer - St. Thomas.

A group of boys playing hockey on a pond.
Two little boys collecting eggs.
Miles and miles of water, rock and trees.

Riding the rails around the north shore of Lake Superior. Rock and water and trees. Cold and clammy mist making us shiver. Plenty of speed with a double-header hiking along. White River at seven a.m. A wash in the river and rustling some grub. Five hours waiting while the livestock get their feed. Hopping a boxcar to go to MacTier. Lots to do when I get back home. Build that fence for Mom and Ken. No more free lettuce for the rabbits. No more traipsing around the neighbourhood for the dog. And I'll go in with Charlie on those apples. Good old Ontario apples. A thank-you gift for the Culhams from Charlie and me.

Rode into Toronto on a cattle truck, to the Union Stock yards. Charlie walked on ahead, and Ivan and I kept together. We made 27 miles today and only rode 7. Our feet are badly blistered and quite tender. We ate behind a Church, in a graveyard tonight. And then we slept in the church.

"With the unpredictability of the weather in mind, it is amazing how often our meteorologists are correct in their predictions, with some estimates reaching as high as almost ninety percent."

"Many Canadians feel that the future is not in their hands."

He is riding on the top of a boxcar. Chewing on an apple that he picked across the fence. It was great to go out West, but I would never want to live there. It's a nice place to earn a few dollars, but it isn't home. Not enough water. Too much wind. That wind out there is blowing all the time. You toss a fork-load up on the wagon and it all blows away. And you don't see green out there. I miss the creeks and the forests and the pond in Pinafore Park. Nothing like lying on the beach at Port Stanley in the summer and cooling off in the lake. The perfect way to end a working day. And apples. I love apples. And there isn't a decent apple west of Ontario. If I don't get more work on the railway, I'll get some work on the farms. And I'll buy a hogshead of apples – a whole barrel of apples – hand-picked Spy apples – and ship it out to the Culhams as soon as I can.

See a bit of the world - sat on a rock - waters were parting - burst the grapes - each child holding a dime - lazy and enjoyable day - with his own two hands - rock and water and trees - badly blistered and quite tender - correct 85% of the time.

My father died when I was seven years old. It wasn't a major event. Lots of people's fathers die when they're quite young.

My dad's pay stopped the minute he was injured. Not a dime while they were carrying him home from the wreck. You don't get paid unless you're using your hammer or saw.

My mother was left with five kids. Five kids and not a penny in the world. She got busy and figured a way to pay the bills.

*Rest your eyes
on the valley
far below.*

Raiding an orchard outside of Toronto. Climbing over the fence. Running back to the train and clambering on. Getting my first Ontario apple in the neck. Nearly falling down onto the tracks. Catching myself before I fall. Giving Ivan a piece of my mind. What the hell you think you're doing – throwing that thing? Rather ride with Charlie than Ivan any time. Figuring we'd better not ride much further on the trains. Lots of rumours about the RCMP at Toronto. One fellow showing an ugly scar behind his right ear.

We were on the road at 6:30. We were promised a ride to London, but it didn't materialize. We walked 10 miles this morning to Waterdown just north of Hamilton. For dinner, Ivan extracted a quart of milk from a cow while I humoured her. Our feet are so sore, it is humanly impossible to walk further.

"Astronomers have discovered nine planets which are orbiting around our sun, and it is possible that some observant person might well discover a tenth someday."

He is riding in the back of a livestock truck. He holds his hat in his hand so it doesn't blow away. Left Mom and Ken in a hurry back in June. Didn't have time to fix the fence like I told her I would. So I'll start right in on the fence as soon as I'm home. Be nice to get back on the railroad, but there's plenty of brakemen in line. Hoping they'll need another hand on the carpentry gang. Boxcars, stations, outbuildings. Porches and steps and doors. They fix everything wooden in the railroad yards from St. Thomas all the way to Windsor – and everything that's wooden in between. That's the job I'd like to have of all the jobs on the railroad. Six days a week and a full day's pay every day. Got my dad's tools and some of my own. Working with wood I could really enjoy. Even better than training those colts. There's nothing quite like the grain in a piece of white oak. And someday – maybe a long, long time from now – I'd like to tear the old house down and build me a new one. The truck hits a pothole and he almost takes a tumble. Been in livestock trucks before. Hauled a bull one time with Charlie to the Anderson farm. That one gave us a bit of a challenge. Have to clean off these boots in a hurry. Just as soon as I find me a patch of grass.

Riding in a cattle truck.
Hitchhiking as the sun comes up.

Wasn't a major event - not a penny in the world - figured a way - showing an ugly scar - to fix the fence - a piece of white oak - build me a new one

- more like a brick - leave the thorns - the rest of my life.

Those were the best times of all. When I was seven years old. And waiting at the edge of the gully for my dad to come home.

My brothers and sisters were all together. And my mom would be tending the garden. And supper would be cooking on the stove.

And he'd be carrying his lunch-pail. And he'd put it down in the grass. And he'd swing me up on his shoulders and carry me home.

Where you stand
the waters meet
the waters part.

Riding into Toronto on a cattle truck. Letting us off at the Union Stock Yards. Charlie walking on ahead and Ivan and me hitch-hiking together. Riding seven miles and walking another twenty. Boots beside me on the grass as I rub my feet. So sore it's humanly impossible to walk any further. This *World Book*'s more like a brick than a stack of paper. What a crazy thing to lug it all this way. Eating in a graveyard behind a church. Bedding down on one of the pews. No fire this time, but the walls keep out the cold. Blisters on my feet and tender soles. Telling Ivan to keep it to a whisper if he's going to sing hymns.

11:17 - 11:18 - 11:19 - 11:20 - 11:21 - 11:22 - 11:23 - 11:24 - 11:25 - 11:26 - 11:27 - 11:28 - 11:29 - 11:30 - 11:31- 11:32 - 11:33 - 11:34 - 11:35 - 11:36 - 11:37 - 11:38 - 11:39 - 11:40 - 11:41- 11:42 - 11:43 - 11:44 - 11:45 - 11:46 - 11:47 - 11:48 - 11:49 - 11:50 - 11:51- 11:52 - 11:53 - 11:54 - 11:55 - 11:56 - 11:57 - 11:58 - 11:59.

The roses
on the trellis
are out in bloom.

A wall of water sweeping through a gorge.
A little boy nibbling a biscuit and sipping tea.
A round earth projected onto a flat map.

Go and get mommy
two or three roses
for the vase.

A child of the oblate spheroid?
A child of the universe?
A child of anything but your own fertile brain?

Just the roses
mind you –
leave the thorns.

On the road at six-thirty. Sun coming up as we walk along. Ten miles just to get to Waterdown. Still a long, long way from home. Not one car will give us a lift for even a mile. Paying for a bus to take us to Paris. Just one dime between us for a phone call, so we set out to walk. My feet can't hold out much longer. Soles of my feet feel like they're raw. Sunny day, though. Breeze is nice. Apple orchards on either side. Like to lie down here and relax for the rest of my life. Hey wait a second! Ivan, look! Is this Ken? By God, I hope it is! Looks like it from a distance! Looks like a '27 Chev! Better drop this pack and get out on the highway and flag him down! If it's not him, I'll only be good for a few more miles. Ivan wouldn't know Ken to see him, but I'm sure gonna know! Standing out in the middle of the pavement and waving my arms!

Three Books

Cyril Passfield: Out West – a novel

    In June, 1932, in the depths of the Great Depression, two part-time railway workers, twenty-three year old Cyril Passfield, and his friend, Charlie Thompson, decide to leave their home town, St. Thomas, Ontario. They go 'on the hobo', joining the great army of the unemployed who are riding the trains back and forth across Canada, heading out West to see if they can get work in the harvest, or maybe hop a freighter and see the rest of the world.

The Making of Out West – a reflective journal

    This journal records my reflections on the process of the crafting of the novel as it evolved through the stages of planning, writing, editing and polishing. It constitutes an effort to be as conscious as possible of the process whereby the single idea that suggested the topic of the novel was expanded into a complex work of art. Topics range from the nuts and bolts of novel-building to the nature of the novel as an art-form.

Planning Out West – a planning notebook

    During the writing of the novel, I kept a hand-written notebook which records the day-by-day development of the novel as it found its shape and style. The notebook – now in print form – reveals how a vast cluster of thoughts was sifted, selected, structured and polished into novel-form.

The Project

    Together, this novel, journal and notebook comprise the twenty-first installment in an on-going novel-writing project in which I am exploring the concept of form and meaning in the novel, and of the novel as a form of expression in the 21st Century. All of the published journals and notebooks are available for free download at www.johnpassfield.ca.

About the Author

John Passfield was born in St. Thomas, Ontario, Canada, and continues to reside in Southern Ontario, near Cayuga, with his family. He has taught and studied literature, creative writing and drama, and is interested in the development of the novel as an art-form.

Novels by John Passfield

Grave Song
The Agony of Robert Chisholm

Jumbo
P. T. Barnum's Greatest Creation

Pinafore Park
The Swan Boat Incident

Water Lane
The Pilgrimage of Christopher Marlowe

Rain of Fire
The Ordeal of Conductor Spettigue

Victoria Day
The Fabric of the Community

The Wright Brothers
Flight is Possible

Leni Riefenstahl
The Valley of the Shadow

Babe Ruth
Out of the Park

Raskolnikov
Murder with an Axe

Sergei Eisenstein
Death Day

Albert Einstein
Wonder

Geoffrey Chaucer
Canterbury Bound

Ospringe
A Visit with Grandad

Pompeii
Vesuvius Dominus

Beethoven
The Ninth Immersion

Job
The Cornerstone of the Universe

Bethune
The Only Person Alive in the World

Terry Fox
Somewhere the Hurting Must Stop

Lord and Lady Macbeth
Full of Scorpions Is My Mind

Cyril Passfield
Out West

Glenn Gould
Light and Dark

Emily Brontë
More Myself Than I

See www.johnpassfield.ca for publishing information.

In Search of Form and Meaning: Journals by John Passfield

Each journal is a day-by-day record of the complex process that a writer undergoes while crafting a work of art. It records the largest decisions, of structure and theme, and the smallest decisions, such as the choice of one word over another, and the constant interaction between the two. Each journal is a record of a writer's reflection on the craft of novel-writing.

The Making of Grave Song

The Making of Jumbo

The Making of Pinafore Park

The Making of Water Lane

The Making of Rain of Fire

The Making of Victoria Day

The Making of Flight is Possible

The Making of The Valley of the Shadow

The Making of Out of the Park

The Making of Murder with an Axe

The Making of Death Day

The Making of Wonder

The Making of Canterbury Bound

The Making of Ospringe

The Making of Vesuvius Dominus

The Making of The Ninth Immersion

The Making of The Cornerstone of the Universe

The Making of The Only Person Alive in the World

The Making of Somewhere the Hurting Must Stop

The Making of Full of Scorpions Is My Mind

The Making of Out West

The Making of Glenn Gould: Light and Dark

The Making of Emily Brontë: More Myself Than I

See www.johnpassfield.ca for publishing information.

The Novel as an Art-Form: Planning Notebooks by John Passfield

Each planning notebook is a printed version of the hand-written notebook which records the planning, writing, editing and polishing of each novel. Each notebook is an attempt to record, understand, and organize the vast cluster of thoughts which occur as one grapples with the various levels of organization which a clear yet complex work of art demands.

Planning Grave Song

Planning Jumbo

Planning Pinafore Park

Planning Water Lane

Planning Rain of Fire

Planning Victoria Day

Planning Flight is Possible

Planning The Valley of the Shadow

Planning Out of the Park

Planning Murder with an Axe

Planning Death Day

Planning Wonder

Planning Canterbury Bound

Planning Ospringe

Planning Vesuvius Dominus

Planning The Ninth Immersion

Planning The Cornerstone of the Universe

Planning The Only Person Alive in the World

Planning Somewhere the Hurting Must Stop

Planning Full of Scorpions Is My Mind

Planning Out West

Planning Glenn Gould: Light and Dark

Planning Emily Brontë: More Myself Than I

See www.johnpassfield.ca for publishing information.

www.ingramcontent.com/pod-product-compliance
Lightning Source LLC
Chambersburg PA
CBHW070045120526
44589CB00035B/2321